KEEPING YOUR HOME IN ONE PIECE

KEEPING YOUR HOME IN ONE PIECE

A Common Sense Guide to keeping your
Home in One Piece with A Mortgage Modification

Reuben Dunn

Colima Books

Foreword

The information contained in this book is accurate at the time of printing; however, approval guidelines for both private lender and for Government sponsored modifications, e.g., HAMP/HRUP/HAUP et al, are subject to change without notice. It is recommended that you view the relevant web pages; the addresses that are contained within this book, for any possible updates or changes to lending policy of either the private investor, or the Treasury Departments Making Home Affordable program.

This book is not meant to provide legal opinions or offer legal advice, and is not meant to serve as a substitute for advice by licensed, legal or tax professionals.

The author and publisher shall have no liability or responsibility to any person or entity regarding any loss or damage incurred, or alleged to have incurred, directly or indirectly, by the information contained in this book.

> *It is highly recommended that you seek qualified legal and tax advice for any matters related but not solely limited to short sale, deed in lieu of foreclosure, foreclosure, bankruptcy-active or discharge, as well as any other matter relating to the modification of your mortgage.*

Table of Contents

Preface

In 2007, a financial tsunami of epic proportions hit the worldwide economy and crashed onshore in the United States, violently affecting both the employment community and the housing market.

Within a relatively short period of time, several million homeowners found their property value turned upside down, with their homes eventually ending up being worth hundreds of thousands of dollars less than they were at the time of purchase.

This financial tsunami was going to be a depreciation of the residential property value, as well as an accelerated devaluation that would ultimately reach into every household in the United States of America.

Included within this financial tsunami of underwater mortgages were several million mortgages, commonly known as "sub-prime" that led the way, and focused our attention on the growing numbers of homes at severe risk of foreclosure and repossession.

Many of these sub-prime mortgages, approved by lenders such as Countrywide Mortgages, would be sold to individuals who simply were unable to afford what is considered a traditional mortgage; i.e.,

a mortgage where the principle, interest, taxes, and insurance, are included in the monthly repayment. Millions of Prospective homeowners walked into a sub-prime housing trap from which they would not be able to escape.

These mortgages for the most part were primarily interest repayment mortgages, with a very small component set up for principle balance repayments. These mortgages, for the most part, weren't set up to be totally repaid at the end of their 25-30 year term.

These sub-prime mortgages, coupled with the downturn in the global economy, meant that these once affordable homes weren't so affordable any more.

As a result of these kinds of mortgages being sold, the financial tsunami had hit the United States, and began its destructive damage.

In response to this real estate melt down, the United States Federal Government, along with the majority of the major mortgage lenders, put in place in the latter part of 2008, a system of mortgage loan modifications, which would provide relief in the form of reduced interest payments, contained in the monthly repayments. It would take an enormous attempt to halt the damage that the financial tsunami had caused.

Countrywide Mortgages and similar sub-prime lenders would eventually go out of business, and other lenders, notably Bank of America, would end up buying in bulk the subprime mortgages set up by Countrywide. The inheritance of the sub-prime mortgages, along with the preexisting problems that the banks' conventional homeowners were having, began to cause a massive bottleneck of work for the Home Retention Departments of the major mortgage lenders.

In response to the escalating crisis, the United States Treasury Department implemented a rescue plan, which would be known as the Home Affordable Modification Program (HAMP). This program was established to provide relief to distressed homeowners by reducing mortgage repayments either by amortization onto the outstanding principle balance, or by reducing the interest rate and then placing the outstanding balance at the end of the mortgage on an interest free balloon basis. This new HAMP program would not be without its own growing problems however.

With both the banks and the Treasury Department putting into place various modification programs, they found themselves under siege, as literally millions of homeowners, would seek help in reducing their repayments and interest rates in the hopes of keeping their homes.

For over four years, while working at Bank of America, I have had the opportunity to take part in this rehabilitation process, beginning with my working in the Home Retention Department for the first year and a half, and then transitioning into a new department that worked out of the Office of the President and CEO. This department was established due to the number of customer complaints about either the delay in modification, appeals for declines, requests for a second look or anyone of another half dozen inquires that went directly to the President of the bank.

While working within the Office of President and CEO, one of the tasks I had was in making initial contact with the homeowners within one hour of being sent their email complaint. It was my responsibility to smooth over the rough spots and to see what, if anything we could do to assist the homeowners.

As my time in the bank lengthened, I became more and more aware that the majority of the homeowners that I had spoken to simply did not know how the modification process was meant to work; many assuming that this was just going to be the same as a full bore refinance of their mortgage.

I found that the majority of the homeowners were basing their knowledge about the modification process from second, or even third hand information that they had heard either from a friend or from an internet web page.

Some of those who had a third party representative work on their behalf weren't given the entire explanation of the "Whys" and "Wherefores" of the modification process. I attributed this lack of knowledge to three key areas:

1. Poor customer service on the part of our staff, sometimes, when dealing with a high volume of customers. Prior to my transfer to the Office of the President, I had a customer pipeline of over one hundred, and we didn't always take the necessary time to fully explain the good, bad, and the ugly bits of the modification process.

2. The third party representatives, some of them at least, didn't clearly explain what they would be able to do on behalf of the homeowner. Some third party representatives tended to put their own interests in front of the homeowner, and, as a result presented, at best, a skewed version of how the process works, and at worst, made out right misstatements (lies in other words) on what they, the 3rd party advocate would get us (The Bad Guys) to do for their clients' mortgage.

3. The final reason, I think, for this lack of knowledge, came as a result of the fluidity of changes to the modification process in the beginning days of the crisis.

I can recall in 2009-2010, having hour or two hour training sessions on both the in-house modifications, and HAMP modification guidelines, only to have another meeting that same week, which reversed what was previously supposed to have been set in stone, which took things in a new direction entirely.

The country was, and still is to some extent, in a state of shock as millions of homeowners found themselves with the real certainty of losing their homes on a scale not seen since the Great Depression of the1930's.

Finance officials were trying their best to get ahead of the problem. This was turning into a "learn as you go" environment. We simply did not have the ability to stop all delinquency/foreclosure movement, take a month or three out and get things set up.

Homes were at risk and hemorrhaging had to stop immediately.

During the early days of the modification process, lessons were learned, mistakes corrected, and more people were pressed into service to deal with modifications.

Let me give you an example of what I mean.

When Bank of America had established their Default Service Complaint Resolution Team, there were only a few hundred members of staff, spread out over three offices in three States. By the time I had left the bank in 2012, there were at least four divisions within the credit department of the bank were shut down, with those members of staff being retrained and then assimilated into the loan modification divisions of the bank.

To give you an idea of the size of the caseload that we were working on, there were over two thousand members of staff working on escalated complaints alone. Now, if each of us had a customer work base of between 40-80 customers, multiply that by 2000 Account Managers, and you'll get an idea of what we were up against. Keep in mind this did not take into account the modifications that were not part of my department.

Take 1000 employees and give them 90-100 customers each, in only one building in Southern California, and you'll get an idea of the scope of damage that the mortgage crisis had brought about.

So why did I feel that I had to write this book?

As I mentioned earlier; I became aware of the factual lack of information that homeowners were being given, either by some members of staff, from the internet, or sad to say, by the very advocates that they were paying fees to do their modifications, in many instances paying amounts between $2000.00-$8000.00. Those that got their information from the internet were not that much better off either.

I recently did an internet search on loan modification web sites to see how many were still online. I found several dozen websites, still active, but that are still using outdated information from 2008, 2009, and 2010. Using this kind of information is risky at best, and should be of concern to anyone seeking to remain in their home.

I wanted to put down onto paper the "Whys" and "Why Not's" of the loan modification process. As you read this book:

- We'll look at what programs the Federal Government has in place for loan modifications and what the eligibility requirements are. We will see what assistance they can provide to distressed homeowners who lose their homes due to foreclosure.

- How does the in-house modification process work, and is it as good a deal as the HAMP programs? While each lender will do the process differently, the basics are universal, e.g., what documentation is needed, what are the financial requirements for approval etc.

- What about the foreclosure and Bankruptcy processes; what will be the long-term effects of entering into either of these two processes?

- We'll also look at whether or not you really need someone to work on your behalf to do the modification, as well as what they can they do that you can't?

In order to help you better understand what forms may be required to fill out during the modification process, I have included example forms for at the end of this book.

I've also included web page addresses for you to use that will enable you to print out those forms on your own. These can also be found in the Appendix section of this book.

Two charts for your reference are also included. One chart listing the lenders in the United States that are, as of June 2013, taking part with the Treasury Department's HAMP modification program, as well as the linking web page address for you to review to get current updated information. The second chart is a breakdown map of the States that are Judicial and Non Judicial insofar as the foreclosure process, of all fifty States. The chart will also give brief explanations of what Judicial and Non Judicial mean.

It is hoped that the information contained in this book will help you understand how the modification process works, as well as giving you a better insight into the reasons of why your modification request was granted or declined.

One final thing; this book is not meant to be an all-inclusive manual for doing a loan modification. Each lender has their own processes for determining modification eligibility; however, the book will provide you with the essentials of the home modification process, as well, what you can expect during the modification review, and decision-making process.

Reuben Dunn
Sandy Utah
October 2015

What is the Process to Qualify for a Loan Modification

One of the major complaints that occurs from time to time, is that some homeowners are told that their accounts have to be delinquent a certain amount of time, usually 90 days, before they can be reviewed for modification assistance.

This means they would have to intentionally place their mortgages in a delinquent state, as well as risk lowering their FICO credit score. The reasoning of this is not generally fully explained by either the lenders, or third party advocates.

The reasoning behind this forced delinquency is due to the face that there are investors who, as a matter of policy, will not allow a modification to be reviewed unless there is a demonstrable form of hardship, in the form of missed payments.

In the early days, this would mean that the homeowners who were up to date with their mortgage payments would need to let their accounts go into three-month arrears before help would even be considered. This caused no end of problems both for the homeowner, as they had to watch their credit score begin to take a nose dive, as well as for the lenders when word got out that banks and lenders were telling their customers to let the account default before they could do anything.

After a year or so of the policy being adhered to, the Treasury Departments HAMP program, in 2010, along with a majority of investors, will now make an allowance for up to date accounts, and will allow applications to be made under the "Imminent Default" category.

Imminent Default simply means that while the account may be current this month, the homeowner has a demonstrable hardship that shows that meeting these payments is not financially viable on an ongoing basis, and that help needs to be given immediately. More and more lenders are allowing for Imminent Default.

However, if the homeowner did not qualify for Imminent Default, either through HAMP or through an in-house modification, they then have to make the decision on whether or not to allow the mortgage payments to go into arrears so that they can meet the investor guidelines of verifiable hardship.

There is a very fine line between telling your customer not to pay until the account is 90 days past due, and telling them what the investor guidelines are in that particular instance, and then letting them make whatever decision they wish.

It's not a perfect system, but at the moment it's what there is.

This conversation however, in my experience, did not come up that often for either my colleagues or me. The vast majority of the modifications that I've worked on over a 4 year period were accounts that were 3, 9, 12 18, and, in more than a few cases, over 48 + months past due.

Payment to Income

So, what about the actual method of calculation that's used for a loan modification; how is it determined whether or not a particular loan is eligible for modification assistance? Is it really that difficult?

A lot of the time the term "Payment to Income" is used, either on the internet, the application, or when it's discussed with me over the phone. What does it mean? What is it exactly? How does it affect the final determination?

Payment to income ratio is the main calculation that underwriters will use in determining whether or not a loan modification is financially viable for the lender to modify the terms and conditions of the mortgage, as well as their determining whether or not this is an affordable solution for the homeowner.

The calculation involves using the monthly gross income from your pay check, against a percentage scale of between 31-42%, a standard that the United States Department of the Treasury has set for the Making Home Affordable Program. For clarification purposes we need to note that the definition of Gross Income is the amount of money earned before taxes and withholding are removed.

Let's take a basic example of how debt to income is calculated; then let's put together a scenario to see how this works, as well as what could be done to help things along.

Doing the payment to income calculation first of all is rather a simple matter. All you need to do is to take your monthly gross (pre-tax) income and multiply it by 31%, by 0.31. The end result of this calculation being 31% of your monthly income. This is the maximum amount that the government thinks you should spend on an affordable monthly mortgage payment, which will tend to also include the cost of insurances and property taxes.

The Review Process

What does the review process entail and how is this payment to income calculated? Let's look at the following example:

Let's suppose that the total gross income for the mortgage holder is $3000.00. Remember, this income is your monthly gross (before taxes). Now, 31 (31%) of this income is calculated to be $930.00. Under the lending guidelines of the loan modification program the lender would need to bring in the modified monthly payment to $930.00 or less.

If, after doing the necessary additional calculations, which we'll look at in a second, the underwriter is not able to put together a modification using that $930.00 as a bench mark, the modification will be declined for something that is known as "Excessive Forbearance".

Excessive Forbearance

Excessive Forbearance simply means that a modification proposal is not available, due to the lender having to change the terms of the loan beyond the requirements of the program. Simply put, the lender would have to do a complete refinance/rewrite of the mortgage, which is outside of the scope of the modification program.

Is there a way to get around this decline? Yes, there can be.

Most modification requests come from mortgage holders where there is only a single signee. Even though Mr. and Mrs. are living in the home, there is only one signature on the mortgage. There's only one person in that household who is recognized as being responsible for the mortgage payments. In these instances, if there is more than one person in the household who is bringing in a pay check, that 2nd person would be invited to submit his/her pay slips alongside of the mortgage signee. That 2nd person would not be required to sign any paperwork, nor would they be responsible for any of the ongoing mortgage payments.

Depending on the lender, however, what may be required would be, in addition to the pay slips, the submission of bank statements (unless there's a joint bank account) that would cover up to the most recent 60 consecutive days. This is so the underwriter can determine what other financial commitments that person has, and if the inclusion of those pay details would put not only the modified mortgage payments at risk, but any additional credit commitments that person has.

So, if we take both pay slips into consideration, the modified target of 31% is generally attainable.

In addition to pay slips being used as a source of income, what about rent? Are you a landlord? Are you renting out a room in your home for extra money? Do your college age kids live with you, and do they pay room and board? If so, you can use this as a source of income.

In this instance you will need to provide a lease/rental agreement, signed and dated, that contains the address of the rental property, even if it's a room in your house, the total monthly rent as well as the payment date. The rental agreement can be either in the form of a handwritten agreement or a formal formatted one. Boilerplate agreements can be obtained at most office supply stores such as Staples and Office Max.

You will need to provide proof of a minimum of the most recent 60 days consecutive rental payments, of cancelled checks, front and back, or proof of deposit on your most recent 60 days consecutive bank statements.

WARNING: If your rent is paid to you in cash, DO NOT use that money to pay the bills, buy food, or fill up the gas tank in the car, and then deposit the remainder. If you get $800.00 a month in rent, the underwriting people will need to see that exact amount deposited into your bank account. Buy the food etc., AFTER you make the deposit, NOT before.

Do you get monthly Social Security-Disability benefits? This can be used for income too. Each year the Treasury Department issues a letter of entitlement to those who are receiving benefits. This letter will tell you how much you will be getting on a monthly basis.

Do you receive a monthly pension or annuity? If so, you would likewise need to submit a similar statement as part of the document submission process. It will help the review process if you were able to also submit a letter, written on company stationery, from the pension or annuity provider that discloses how long the payments to you will be for.

Along with submitting the needed income verification, what else is used to determine eligibility? While the process does vary from lender to lender, you can count on the following documents and areas to be reviewed at during the application process:

- Original Outstanding Balance
- Current Unpaid Principle Balance
- Any Principle Balance Reduction
- Total Amount Past Due
- Number of Payments Past Due
- Total Past Due Amount Reduced (if allowed by investor.)
- Current Interest Rate
- Total Gross Income Zip Code
- FICO (Credit) Score

- Is there a bankruptcy involved; has it been discharged?
- What percentage 31-42% is being used for the calculation
- Single or joint income

The process of a modification review is rather straight forward at the end of the day, as the process will simply provide a yes or no response, based on the financial documentation that is submitted.

The guidelines from both the Federal Government's HAMP program, as well as guidelines of the particular mortgage investor are rather clear and uniform in content.

As long as the information provided to the lender is accurate and not "massaged" in any way by the homeowner at the point of submission, this will give both the Lender and the Homeowner an accurate financial picture on whether or not a home loan modification is viable or not.

The adage "Numbers don't Lie" is a truism and comes into play during the modification process

ARE THE LENDER GUIDELINES SET IN STONE?

Take two identical houses in a residential area. They're the same height, shape, color, square footage and have the same mortgage lender. Many would assume that if the Bank of New York is the mortgage holder on both house 'A' and house 'B' then they both should be eligible for modification assistance right? Not necessarily.

While both homes in the example are mortgaged by the Bank of New York, the mortgages may not be the same type. The Bank of New York has over 100 different mortgages that banks service on their behalf, and each mortgage will have differing terms and conditions attached to them. Each one will be geared towards the customer that fits, for example, a pre-determined income level, a credit score level, etc.

So even though your friend next door has a home that is financed by the Bank of New York, just like yours their mortgage may not allow for any modifications done to it because of the type of mortgage that they have. Their credit score may not be identical to yours. There is no single "one–size-fits-all" mortgage.

Many investors, for example, may not participate with HAMP. The investor may not allow the interest rate to be reduced or the repayment term to be extended. Some investors also not allow for any sort of modification to the mortgage at all, other than perhaps an amortization of the outstanding balance on to the current unpaid principle balance. What this will mean, of course, is that while the account will become current, the interest rate will not change, and the monthly repayment will tend to increase.

Some of the mortgages that are being reviewed are deemed as too much of a credit risk for that investor to allow for a modification. When one looks at a mortgage that hasn't been paid in over 36-48-60 months, the balance outstanding is too high, and there is no way for that investor to recoup the monies lost already.

Insofar as eligibility is concerned, there simply is no clean cut answer beforehand as to who can/cannot receive modification assistance; it depends both on the accuracy of the documentation that is submitted by the homeowner, as well as what direction is given from the mortgage holder.

Remember, the offering of HAMP and Loan Modifications are NOT mandatory on the part of the lenders, and there are lenders who don't think that the financial risk is great enough to pursue any sort of modification.

Will the mortgage investor lose money on this mortgage investment by not doing a loan modification? Well, to tell the truth, they already have. Keep in mind that in the vast majority of modification requests made, the lenders will have not been paid for some time, in some cases, for well over three years.

Depending on the type of mortgage, the balance outstanding, and the area that the house is located, some lenders that I know will suggest a Short

Sale or a Deed in Lieu of Foreclosure, rather than risk doing a modification, simply because the house is in an area with rental housing.

The investors can get the property back, put it into shape if need be, and then rent it out for a period of time until the housing prices and economy get back to where they belong.

Let's look at what will tend to happen if there is an approval for a modification for either the Making Home Affordable Program, or for an in-house modification.

If you've been approved for HAMP/In-House Modification eligibility, you may be put on a three month trial payment basis. This is a litmus test of affordability. If there are any repayment issues with the modification, they will generally come to the surface within the first three months of the modification. During this time your credit report will continue to show a delinquency, however the reporting would be classified as 'U' for unknown; that is to say, you're not current, nor are you delinquent. Credit reports are fixed against the contractual payments at the time of signing.

It is important to note that should you default on any of the trial payments, you can be removed from the modification program entirely and be rejected from any subsequent reapplication. It is strongly encouraged that you keep in contact with your lender during this process and let them know if there are problems with the repayments. They can re-exam the submitted documentation if need be, and issue new paperwork if it's found that there might be a better repayment plan for you.

Remember, this is what the trial period is set up for; it's a period of time to see what repayment problems, if any, may crop up, as well as finding out if there are solutions to these problems.

If there are any repayment problems at this point, they may not be solvable, and you could easily be told that there are no other modification options available for you. This is what the trial payments are for; to assess both the commitment level of the homeowner, as well as to see if the solution is as practical in real life as it is on paper.

I cannot emphasize strongly enough the need to submit 100% accurate financial and income documentation during the application process.

Once the third payment is received, you should then be sent permanent modification documents to review, sign, notarize and return. Once this happens, and the paperwork is processed, your credit report will be amended to reflect the new payments, and you effectively start out with a new loan. The delinquent payments tend to be removed from the credit report within the first 90-120 days, although if the account has been in a delinquent state for a while, it may take a bit longer for them to be removed.

Keep in mind that in the event that a modification is not possible, either due to investor prohibition, or due to affordability problems, on the part of the homeowner, the direction of the conversation between homeowner and modification specialist, will usually take a different direction. The shift will tend to go from that of home retention to that of debt liquidation, i.e., the disposal of the property via short-sale, or via a voluntary return of the keys through the Deed in Lieu of Foreclosure process.

We'll go through each of these processes, as well as a brief look at the foreclosure process later on in the book.

The framework described above is generally used industry wide; although, as mentioned before, many lenders, and even some HAMP applications, will do away with the three month trial period altogether. In this case it is extremely important to be 100% committed to meeting the monthly repayment obligations, as defaulting on any payments may prohibit further modification assistance from being given for at least twelve months. Some mortgage lenders will state that a default on the modification payment at all would mean that no further mortgage modifications would be done.

Again, If you have any concerns about the repayments being proposed, the time to question them is before you submit any signed modification agreement.

How long will it take for the review to begin? While the time frame will differ from each lender, the larger lenders, Chase, Wells Fargo, and Bank of America, for example, will generally tell their customers that from the time that all documentation is received, to the process of review may take a minimum of 6 weeks. The best thing you can do at this point is to make sure either you, or your advocate, calls them up regularly, one every two weeks for example, for updates.

ARE THIRD PARTY ADVOCATES NECESSARY?

Should you get outside help in application for a mortgage modification? Is it necessary? What company or organization does one approach for help?

In many ways getting these questions answered correctly is just as an important part of the modification process, as the actual modification itself. A poorly made decision can not only run the risk of ruining any modification prospects, but it can also create an additional financial hardship as many existing companies, mainly law firms, will charge retainer fees of anywhere from $2000.00-$8000.00.

In the early days of the modification crisis, many companies seemed to crop up overnight, most charging their customers upfront fees, promising the moon, virtually guaranteeing a loan mortgage modification sight unseen. This was a new area and there were few regulations set in place to prevent fraudulent practices such as this. The damage caused by these companies was not immediate.

It was only after the modification documents were submitted to the lenders, that the problems began to creep in. Many of these modification companies would take in huge amounts of money, and then simply fade into the woodwork. I've had many conversations with homeowners over the years who were victims of this kind of dishonesty. They all had lost several thousands of dollars, money that most could not afford to spend in the first place. Fortunately, in most of these instances, I was able to effect a modification for them.

One national organization, The Homeownership Preservation Foundation, belongs to a coalition of public and private agencies that maintain a national database of loan-modification complaints. The Foundation reported that since March 2010, some 28,000 homeowners have reported potential fraud. Their reported monetary losses total around $66 million.

In 2009, the California State Senate passed Senate Bill 94 (SB94), which prohibited the collection of upfront fees to conduct loan modifications. The law was originally set to expire on January 1, 2014, but due to the large numbers of distressed homeowners, the California Senate passed SB980, which extended the SB94 until January 1st, 2017.

This meant that the majority of those mortgage modification companies would no longer be legally allowed to charge any up-front fees; they weren't able charge customers "Processing Fees" or "Administrative Fees". They would only be able to charge a fee once the loan modification process was completed. Given that the time frame is anywhere from 3-6 months, this meant that many companies closed the doors due to no income being generated.

There is an exception to this prohibition of upfront fees. Law firms, who did loan modifications as part of their practice, would be allowed to charge their normal retainer fees to the homeowners who sought assistance.

But even with this exception, there are law firms who are caught with their hands in the cookie jar. A January 10, 2013 New York Times article in the Real Estate Section, reveals how diabolical this practice is. The article revealed that a consumer advocate group had:

"…filed a lawsuit in Suffolk County, New York, alleging that a series of companies run by Rory M. Alarcon, a lawyer licensed in New York, defrauded 17 homeowners out of tens of thousands of dollars. The suit claims that the companies promised owners loan modifications and lower mortgage payments in return for thousands upfront. "To our knowledge, no one received the services that they were promised," said Ms. Mullenbach, who works on the panel's Fair Housing and Fair Lending Project.

"Only three of the homeowners suing Mr. Alarcon live in New York; the rest are scattered across nine states. They are claiming losses from $2,500 to $8,000 apiece.

"These are not individuals who are unsophisticated — some have been extremely well educated," Ms. Mullenbach said. "But they were looking for solutions for how to save their homes."

"…This is the seventh modification-fraud lawsuit the Lawyers' Committee has filed in Long Island since 2011. Three of the other lawsuits also involve lawyers…"

So what you do to avoid being scammed by these kinds of companies?

Two words immediately come to mind: "*Due Diligence*". Do your homework.

One of the warning signs mentioned in the New York Times article has to do with the ratio of modification clients a law firm will have in comparison to the other types of client cases that they handles. As the article states:

"…when you go to a lawyer and his sole business deals with loan modification, that's a real signal…"

I recall working with a half dozen customers who were living in different parts of the country who were dealing with a law firm that was located in Utah. It turns out that this law firm only dealt with loan modifications. In the spring of 2012 the FBI raided the firm and would ultimately close the firm down due to severe deceptive practices.

When considering working with a law firm whose sole source of business is mortgage modifications, do your homework.

Ask them about what the ratio of the modification side of the practice is to any other areas of the law that they may practice.

Ask them about the fees and charges that you will eventually have to pay. Ask them what alternatives they may be able to suggest should you fail to qualify for a loan modification; will they, for example, be there for you should you need to place the house on the market for a short sale?

Ask as many detailed questions as you can about the level of service that they will give to you.

Remember, should you decide to retain one of these firms to assist with your modification, they work for you.

They should be held as accountable to you as you are to your mortgage lender in making arrangements to bring your mortgage account current.

You need to be able to feel that the people you hire to work on your behalf are working to protect your own interests, instead of its reputation.

Let me give another example of what I mean.

A home was scheduled for a foreclosure sale date about a month and a half before I contacted them. The homeowners had effectively gone to ground and had apparently decided not to seek a way out of their problems. At the time I was given this file, my role was, in effect, to track the process. However, after seeing that no contact was made with the homeowners for some time, I made a last ditch effort to speak with them to see if they wanted to avoid the foreclosure process by doing some sort of modification, or, if they wanted to keep their financial problems out of the public domain by doing a voluntary surrender of the property via the Deed in Lieu of Foreclosure process.

After spending 30 minutes on the phone with the homeowner, it was determined that due to a strange reluctance on his part to submit the financial documentation that I needed to review, that we were not able to proceed any further.

We parted company politely, after I informed him of what the process of foreclosure was, and after I gave him both my contact details, and assurances that we, the company I worked for, wanted to see if we could avoid the foreclosure process by either a modification, or a Deed in Lieu, which would have a far lesser impact on their credit score. We hung up and I went on to work with other homeowners.

Two weeks later I got an email from a law firm that was now representing the homeowner. The email contained a letter from the attorney requesting that we reduce the interest rate to 2%, forgive the back payments, the homeowner was nearly 3 years delinquent, along with our doing a principle reduction balance of over $100.000.00. They also wanted us to amend their credit score to reflect that the account was no longer in arrears. In short, they wanted us to give away the store entirely.

Letters like this, while unrealistic, actually serve two purposes. First, I feel that they're really written for their client's benefit, perhaps showing them how tough the attorney can be with the mortgage lender. The second reason for these types of letters has more to do with that advocate setting up a starting point with the mortgage company.

It's akin to putting the first shot across the bow, or testing the waters. In over 4 years of doing mortgage modifications, and getting these sorts of letters, I have never heard of anyone taking these kinds of letter seriously.

However, the letter was serious, and the clock was ticking. I had to make contact with the attorney's office to see what we could do to avoid the foreclosure sale date.

This was not going to be an easy task, as emails and phone messages were not responded to. I began to have some serious questions about this law firm, and their lack of response. Doing a bit of due diligence of my own I did a bit of research on this firm and found that their sole practice was mortgage modifications This raised a warning flag for me..

Finally, after close to a week of calls I finally was able to speak with an attorney. The problem was that during this time the house is still edging towards a foreclosure sale date. After speaking with him for a few minutes, I found to my dismay that he was 100% serious about his proposal/demand on the email he had sent to me.

This alone was bad enough. The main problem was that he was not willing to provide me with any sort of documentation that we needed in order to determine whether the homeowner was even eligible for a loan modification.

We were stuck at an impasse. Even though he was aware that the foreclosure sale date could not be postponed until we could verify eligibility for assistance, he stood his ground and refused to provide me with anything.

When I told him that we were not able to proceed, his words to me were, "Fine, we'll let it go into foreclosure, the courts will tie it up for another year, and at least this way they can still live in the home."

I reminded him of the fact that the homeowner's personal financial business would become a matter of public record, and that his credit record would suffer some additional long-term damage because of this decision. He was not interested in this, and did not want me to communicate with the homeowner about this.

The man was putting his "Hard-as-Nails" reputation ahead of the interests of the homeowner.

I said that under the present circumstances, we would not be able to do anything.

A few days later, I got a call from the homeowner, who asked me for an update.

I asked him if he had spoken with his representative. He said that he had not, and that he was not able to speak with anyone from the firm, as his messages were not being returned.

After asking him if I could speak with him about his account, and getting his consent, I brought him up to speed with both the content of the letter that was sent to us, as well as details of our conversation.

I said that even though the sale date was less than 10 days away, we still could have it postponed, if he wanted to remain in the house, but that we needed the verification of income, and other documents in order to do the review. I said that there was no guarantee that we could even do a modification; but that we could at least buy some time while I did the review.

He agreed to work with me directly, revoked the authorization for the attorney, and we ended up postponing the foreclosure while we did the review process.

I want to make one thing clear however. Not all law firms are like these two. For every two firms who practice like this, I have found several dozen who are reputable, communicative, and who keep in contact on a regular basis, both with me (the lender) and with their/my client. While they do charge a fee, they make no illusions or any false promises of guaranteed modifications, reduced repayment or interest rates.

Do your homework. Check what their practice is actually like.

Be aware of the following warning signs:

- Do they make promises to you that they will 100% be able to keep, e.g., guarantee a modification, reduction in repayment, reduction in interest, forgiveness of all back payment, reduction in principle balance?

- Do they, after taking your financial details and expenses tell you that you qualify for a loan modification?

If they do, then **RUN** not walk, to the nearest exit. <u>No outside firm, public or private, can guarantee a loan modification</u>. As we have seen one, lender may have over 100 different mortgages in their portfolio, and yours may not even qualify for modification assistance.

One final thing - ask that law firm if they can put you in contact with some of their clients that they have worked with and with whom they are working. Reach out to the customers and see what they think of the service that they are paying for.

Do your homework; odds are you're going to be paying several thousand dollars that you may not have, for them to do something that can, and is, easily done by yourself.

The Treasury Department, on their Making Home Affordable web page www.makinghomeaffordable.gov, has the following four things to be aware of in determining whether the company offering you help with your mortgage modification is a scam outfit or not:

Beware of anyone who asks you to pay a fee in exchange for counseling services for the modification of a delinquent loan.

Beware of people who pressure you to sign papers immediately or who try to convince you that they can "save" your home if you sign or transfer over the deed to your house.

Do not sign over the deed to your property to any organization or individual unless you are working directly with your mortgage company to forgive your debt.

Never make a mortgage payment to anyone other than your mortgage company without their approval.

The U.S. Department of Housing and Urban Development (HUD) will also provide at no cost to homeowners, advisors who will assist them with services such as:

- Financial Management/Budget Counseling
- Financial, Budgeting and Credit Repair Workshops
- Home Improvement and Rehabilitation Counseling
- Default Resolution Counseling and Workshops
- Delinquency Resolution Counseling and Workshops
- Non-Delinquency Post Purchase Workshops
- Pre-purchase Counseling

- Pre-purchase Homebuyer Education Workshops
- Rental Housing Counseling
- Rental Housing Workshops
- Services for Homeless Counseling

Their web site has inks to their regional and local offices. The address is: http://www.hud.gov/offices/hsg/sfh/hcc/hcs.cfm

There is also a non-profit organization called NACA, which stands for the Neighborhood Assistance Council of America, which generally works with low-income families who have subprime mortgages and who are in need of modification assistance.

Their web page https://www.naca.com states that NACA has:

"...legally binding agreements with all the major lenders/servicers and investors (i.e. Fannie Mae and Freddie Mac) covering approximately 90% of homeowners to achieve to a restructure or forbearance....All of NACA's services are Free. Many...homeowners. Have had their mortgages restructured with interest rates reduced to 4%, 3% and as low as 2% and where necessary the outstanding principal reduced. Homeowners often save over $500 a month and some over $1,000 a month.

"NACA's operational budget comes from mortgage brokerage fees, real estate brokerage commissions and member dues [source: NACA]. The group gets a fee of about $2,000 per loan, which is paid by the lender. The money to provide the loans comes from partnerships with other lending institutions. Bank of America and Citigroup are two of the organization's biggest partners..."

According to its own web page, NACA has about $10 billion in commitments from banks to write loans. The organization provides the screening and counseling, and the bank provides the money.

I have worked rather closely with several NACA related mortgages and can state that, aside from HUD, they are extremely efficient and getting the job done.

They have outdoor events across the country, with the major players attending, Bank of America, Chase, etc., and decisions on modifications are generally made on the spot. Many times the three month trial period is waived as well. I would suggest you take a look at their web site to see what help they might be able to offer.

There is one final point to consider, and that is that with the exception of NACA, due to their agreements with the major lenders in the country; there is nothing that these law firms and modification companies do, that you, as a homeowner, cannot do yourself.

The modification process is exactly the same, the lending requirements remain fixed, and the time frame for completion unchanged. The main difference being that of time management; they have the time, in theory to make the necessary follow up calls that you might not have.

What Documents are Needed for a Loan Modification?

So, what paperwork is generally needed for a modification? While each lender may have their own requirements, the following documents are most likely to be asked for at some point during the review process.

Not all lenders will ask for the same paperwork however. Bank of America, for example, will usually ask for full IRS 1040s for the last tax year, with all schedules and attachments, in addition to a tax statement request form. Another companies will only ask for a 4506-T/T ez tax statement request form. It's best to have these documents on hand, in any event, should your lenders underwriters require any subsequent documentation.

Over the next few pages, we'll look at these documents to see what they are used for.

Letter of Hardship

What is a letter of hardship, and why is it important? Do a Google search about the Letter of Hardship and you're sure to find many opposing points of view about both the need for these letters, and what they should contain. Over the past 4 years I have read literally hundreds of Letters of Hardship. Many were written in long hand, poorly spelled, as well as multipage letters, some typed in single spaced format, providing the entire history of that particular family, including medical history, types of medical treatments taken, etc.

I have also read many single page, two paragraph letters. So, which one is better? Does the formal typewritten letter get a better response/review than a poorly spelled handwritten letter?

Many people will tell you that you have to do this letter "properly" and that that you have to send in a typewritten letter, filled with emotive "facts" as to the reasons of the delinquency, details into the heath history of the family member who has taken ill etc.

Many enterprising people have set up shop, selling what is essentially a boilerplate, fill-in-the-blank letter, and selling them from between $20-30.00 for a single template.

I can't tell you the numbers of letters that I've read that contain the exact same wording as this one which is found on several web sites:

To Whom It May Concern:

I am writing this letter to explain my unfortunate set of circumstances that have caused us to become delinquent on our mortgage. We have done everything in our power to make ends meet but unfortunately we have fallen short and would like you to consider working with us to modify our loan. Our number one goal is to keep our home and we would really appreciate the opportunity to do that.

The reason that I am behind on my mortgage is (explain the reason here as concisely as possible—don't take pages to do so. The reason should be critical, i.e. health related, or trouble feeding a family, a lost job, or so on). I fully intend to pay what I owe on the house, but I have no income through which to do so, as you can see. I believe this situation to be (temporary or permanent) because of (reasons). You can help me by giving me a loan modification. Please (lower my interest rate, reduce my monthly payments to x amount, etc.). See below the balance sheet of my monthly income and expenses.

As you can see, if you granted my loan modification request, I would be able to afford my mortgage and never miss a payment again.

Thank you for your consideration. With your help, I can move on with my life and pay you what I owe.

Sincerely,

(Name, signature and date)

The overall reaction to reading boilerplate letters similar to the one above, has generally been mostly one of sad amusement, and puzzlement on the part of my colleagues and myself.

Reading these same formatted letters, for over four years, made me ask myself why so many people were either spending money on a formatted letter, or doing a cut and paste job from an anonymous web writer, that really served no real purpose in determining whether or not a homeowner qualifies for a loan modification.

Another type of Letters of Hardship that are sent in, are included within documentation that sent in by the third party working for the homeowner.

These kinds of letters not only contain the reasons for the hardship, but a proposal that is usually unrealistic, e.g., asking for automatic reduction of the interest rate to 2%, forgiveness of all missed payment, and a rather sizable reduction in the principle balance. Such verbiage generally is referred to in these letters as the advocates' proposal.

As I mentioned in the last chapter, these kinds of letters are in my opinion, purely written for the benefit of homeowner, as a possible example of how "strong" or proactive that advocate will be. In my experience, such "proposals" are not worth the paper that they are written on, as those who are making such requests, the so-called, "Professionals", more times than not, will simply have no idea what the particular investor guidelines are for loan modifications.

The majority of mortgage investors, for example, will not allow for any forgiveness of either the back payments, or a reduction in the outstanding principle balance. While such things do happen occasionally, they are more the exception rather than the rule. The maturity dates on delinquent mortgages will not be extended either, as it would mean rewriting the whole terms and conditions of the original mortgage, which is beyond the scope of the modification process.

What should your letter of hardship contain?

When asking for a Letter of Hardship, I've advised the homeowner that it should contain two paragraphs at the most, explaining the reasons behind the delinquency, e.g., illness in the family, reduction of work hours, and loss of work.

There is no need to dramatize the circumstances or go into detail, graphic or otherwise, about the medical procedure that has taken place. All is needed is a brief explanation of the "Whys" of the missed payments.

The other paragraph should outline your intentions towards the property: Do you want to remain in the home, or are you looking to do a voluntary surrender of the property? Do you see this problem as being short-term/long-term, or has that problem been resolved at this point in time.

That's all there is to it. Short, Direct, and to the point.

Bank of America, for example, has a sample form that can be found in the Appendix at the end of this book.

Verification of Income

W2 Employees - You will be asked to provide proof of your income in the form of at least the last full 30 days monthly pay slips. This requirement is for a full calendar month. If you are paid on a weekly basis, then pay slips for all four/five weeks of the most recent month would be required. If you are paid once a month, then you would be asked to provide pay slips for the most recent two months. If you are paid twice a month, then both pay slips for that month would be required.

1099 – Self Employed - Small business owners or people who do not get a W2 pay slip; are considered contracted employees, who receive 1099 forms. They would be required to provide a signed and dated Profit and Loss Statement, usually covering the most recent quarter. It's also a good idea to provide a year to date Profit and Loss Statement. These Profit and Loss Statements do not need to be done by accountants.

They need to contain the gross income for a particular period. An itemized breakdown of expenses for that particular period would follow, e.g., office rent, supplies, work related expenses. These expenses would be subtracted from the gross balance, and the net balance would be calculated.

Now, for the interesting part. As far as the requirements for self-employed applicants, most lenders will not use your Gross income as part of the application process. It is the NET balance that is used for the gross monthly income. This is why it is important to insure that all figures on that Profit and Loss Statement are correct.

Landlords – Many homeowners either own second properties, or rent out a portion of their home to boarders. In this circumstance, to use the rental income as part of the overall income verification process, you will be asked to provide proof of tenancy, in the form of a signed and dated lease/rental agreement, which is either on a month to month basis, or has at least a full calendar year remaining on the lease at the time of application.

Out of date lease agreements are not accepted and you will be asked to provide a current agreement.

These lease/rental agreements can either be provided in the form of a pre-printed boilerplate that is easily obtainable at any office supply store, e.g., Staples, Office World. They can also be hand written, as long at this hand written agreement is signed and dated by both you as the landlord and by the tenant.

The agreement should list the full postal address of where your tenant is living, even if it is in your home. It should also contain the total rent due, when it is to be paid by, and that it needs to be paid in the form of postal money order or check. Rental payments by cash tend to be excluded because it is nearly impossible to verify that cash deposit in the bank account as coming from the rent.

You would be required to provide proof of rental deposit, either by canceled checks or by verification of deposit via your last most recent two months consecutive bank statement showing deposits for the rent made.

Some landlords will take cash payment for their rental payment. This can cause a lot of problems if the full cash rental payment is not deposited into the account, before being used to pay the bills, food, etc.

Any balances deposited that is less than the agreed upon monthly rental charge, cannot be verified as rent and will not be used as a source of income.

It is much, much easier from a validation process, to insure that your rent is in the form of a check. Keep in mind also, that many lenders will err on the side of caution and require that your rental payments are paid by check or postal money order. This makes the verification "audit proof" when it comes time for the underwriting process to be done, and the underwriters to validate that the rent on the rental agreement, corresponds with the check deposit in the bank account.

Bank Statements

You'll be asked to provide your most recent bank statements covering a minimum of the most recent 60 consecutive days. All pages are required, front and back of the pages if necessary.

Bank statements are used for a number of reasons. They are used to verify your income. If you're paid on the 15th of the month for a set amount of money, then the modification underwriter will need to be able to track that deposit.

Another reason for the bank statements is that it enables the modification underwriters to also verify the income and expense information, e.g., credit card, car loan repayments, other credit repayments that may not show up during the application process. These statements also give underwriters an opportunity to access the overall spending habits of the homeowners.

Income Tax Verification

IRS Form 1040 - You may be asked, to provide your IRS 1040 tax form, with all schedules and attachments, for the most recent tax year. The schedule "E "report income or loss from rental real estate, royalties, partnerships, S-Corporations, estates, trusts, and residual interests in REMICs (Real Estate Mortgage Investment Conduit). This entity holds a fixed pool of mortgages and issues multiple classes of interests in itself to investors.

In the event you have not filed your most recent tax returns, you will be asked to submit a copy of your form filing a 4868 application for extension.

According to the IRS web page, http://www.irs.gov/uac/Extension-of-Time-To-File-Your-Tax-Return.com, if you haven't filed your taxes in time, you will need to make a request for a tax filing extension. If the extension is granted, you may be able to get an automatic 6-month extension of time to file. For example: If your return is due on April 15, 2013, you will have until October 15, 2013, to file. (Revenue, 2013)

4506-T/4606-T ez - Some lenders ask you to send instead of a 1040, an IRS Form 4506-T/4506-T ez. This is a request for a tax statement, and usually requests statements for the preceding three years. You will be asked to put your postal address that you fill in on the 1040's as well as putting your signature and date on the form. If you file taxes jointly, both parties must fill out the 4606-T/4506-T ez, even if the other party is not on the modification agreement.

It is important to note that many lenders will place a three month viability or shelf life on these 4506-T/4506-T ez forms. Be prepared to re-submit a new form should the review process with the underwriter take longer than two/three months.

Proof of Residence

For MHA/HAMP application, as well as for in-house modifications, you may be asked by your lender to provide a utility bill as proof that you're living at the mortgaged property. Some lenders will accept utility bills that are within 90 days of the application date, although it would be preferable to submit more current utility bills. For clarification purposes, a utility bill could be considered to be electric, gas, phone, cable, local services, e.g., garbage and sewer.

Bankruptcy

If you have filed for Chapter 7 or Chapter 13 protection and have had them discharged, you will be required to provide a certified, court stamped certificate of discharge. You will also need to provide an authorization letter, signed by your bankruptcy attorney, authorizing your lender to speak with you solely concerning the modification aspect of this mortgage. If the bankruptcy is active and ongoing, and should you be approved for a bankruptcy, then the modification agreement would need to be submitted for court approval before any documentation can be issued to you.

Please keep in mind that the courts do have the power to deny the modification application. As has been mentioned before, it is STRONGLY suggested that you seek properly qualified legal counsel from your bankruptcy attorney if you elect to pursue a loan modification.

The Making Home Affordable Program

In 2009, in response to the mortgage crisis, the United States Treasury Department, established a modification program known as Home Affordable Modification Program (HAMP). This program would be used to help those distressed homeowners who through, for the most part, no fault of their own, found themselves in a situation where maintaining their mortgage payments became problematic.

In 2009, there were teething problems with the HAMP/MHA program that had to do with the underwriting process.

In the original application process homeowners would contact their lender by phone, request assistance, and were then asked what their gross monthly income was.

If their stated gross income met the 31% payment to income ratio that the Treasury Department had set, the homeowner would then be placed on a three month trial payment. This was to prevent the home from going into foreclosure.

During that three month period, the homeowner would submit proof of that income, along with other supporting documents. If, at the end of the review, it was determined that the homeowner was not eligible, then they would be declined from further HAMP/MHA assistance.

This process would ultimately create more of a problem than was necessary.

The problem was that those listed on these initial trial modifications had the impression that their problems were solved and that they had a modification in place; after all, they were making their modified monthly repayments as agreed with the banks and lenders. However, when the time came to call them and tell them that they, in fact, were not eligible for the modification, it created an extra degree of tension that didn't need to be there in the first place.

The homeowners who were in this position were not happy and were rightly upset with the banks and with the government, as they had felt that they were being strung along.

Even as late as 2012, there would still be fallout because of the original application process. Thousands of homeowners were placed on that initial three month trial payment, but for some unexplainable reason, a great number of them were not notified of the change in the application process, e.g., sending in documentation first, before the decision process would be made.

These homeowners were not given the opportunity to re-apply. I have spoken with many homeowners who were not informed of this change and were removed from any further modification assistance. Many homeowners eventually end up receiving a Notice of Intent to Default, which is the first step towards foreclosure proceedings.

As recently as 2012, I still received phone calls from homeowners who were still wondering why they were declined for any modification assistance, even though they made the required three months trial period payment, and why they now had a Notice of Default to contend with.

Eventually the Treasury Department temporarily stopped the HAMP/MHA modification process, and came to the realization that it would be better to first gather the documentation, and then determine eligibility, and, if qualified, put the homeowner on the three month trial modification.

HAMP decided to follow the lead of the majority of lenders who required documentation verification first, prior to any decision making process.

Another change made by Federal guidelines was that lenders taking part in the HAMP/MHA program would now be required to offer it first before offering any in-house modification programs. Up until then the HAMP/MHA program was seen as an optional alternative.

After much tweaking of the process, the eligibility requirements have been streamlined to the point that most, if not all of those lenders who are taking part in this program, have aligned their own in-house eligibility requirements to mirror those of the HAMP/MHA program.

In 2015, the Federal Government announced that they would be continuing the HAMP/MHA program until December 31st 2016. This was done to bring these two programs in line with other governmental mortgage assistance programs.

Let's now take a brief look now at the different programs that fall under the MHA program as well as their eligibility requirements.

Home Affordable Modification Program

What are the basic eligibility requirements for HAMP assistance?

- You occupy the house you are calling about as your primary residence.

- Homeowners who are applying for a modification on a home that is not their primary residence, but the property is currently rented or the homeowner intends to rent it

- Your first mortgage is in foreclosure, you are delinquent or default is reasonably foreseeable.

- Your loan closed before January 1, 2009.

- You owe up to $729,750 on your primary residence or single unit rental property

- Your home consists of 4 units or less, and you must occupy one unit.

- You owe up to $934,200 on a 2-unit rental property; $1,129,250 on a 3-unit rental property; or $1,403,400 on a 4-unit rental property

- The property has not been condemned

- You have a financial hardship and are either delinquent or in danger of falling behind on your mortgage payments (non-owner occupants must be delinquent in order to qualify).

- You have sufficient, documented income to support a modified payment.

- Your first mortgage debt-to-income ratio is over 31 percent. Your monthly payment is more than 31persent of your monthly pre-tax income (or your combined monthly income in the case of co-borrowers). In this case, your "monthly payment" includes principal, interest, property taxes, hazard and flood insurance and homeowner owners association due or condominium fees (if applicable). Mortgage insurance payments are not included in this calculation.)

- You can't have been convicted within the last 10 years of felony larceny, theft, fraud or forgery, money laundering or tax evasion, in connection with a mortgage or real estate transaction.

Effective June 1, 2012, the Obama Administration expanded the population of homeowners that may be eligible for the Home Affordable Modification Program to include:

Homeowners who previously did not qualify for HAMP because their debt-to-income ratio was 31% or lower.

Homeowners who previously received a HAMP trial period plan, but defaulted in their trial payments.

Homeowners who previously received a HAMP permanent modification, but defaulted in their payments, therefore losing good standing.

Principal Reduction Alternative (PRA)

If your home is currently worth significantly less than you owe on it, MHA's Principal Reduction Alternative (PRA) was designed to help you by encouraging mortgage servicers and investors to reduce the amount you owe on your home.

You may be eligible for PRA if:

- Your mortgage is not owned or guaranteed by Fannie Mae or Freddie Mac.
- You owe more than your home is worth.
- You occupy the house as your primary residence.
- You obtained your mortgage on or before January 1, 2009.
- Your mortgage payment is more than 31 percent of your gross (pre-tax) monthly income.

- You owe up to $729,750 on your 1st mortgage.
- You have a financial hardship and are either delinquent or in danger of falling behind.
- You have sufficient, documented income to support the modified payment.
- You must not have been convicted within the last 10 years of felony larceny, theft, fraud or forgery, money laundering or tax evasion, in connection with a mortgage or real estate transaction.

Second Lien Modification Program (2MP)

If your first mortgage was permanently modified under HAMP, and you have carry a second mortgage, you may be eligible for a modification or principal reduction on your second mortgage through MHA's Second Lien Modification Program (2MP).

2MP works in tandem with HAMP to provide comprehensive solutions for homeowners with second mortgages to increase long-term affordability and sustainability. If the servicer of your second mortgage is participating, they can evaluate you for a second lien modification.

FHA Home Affordable Modification Program

The FHA, VA and USDA all offer mortgage modification programs for struggling homeowners designed to lower monthly mortgage payment to no more than 31 percent of the homeowner's verified monthly gross (pre-tax) income— making monthly mortgage payments much more affordable. The front-end debt to income ratio on FHA-HAMP programs cannot exceed 40% of the current gross income. This is 2% less than the non-HAMP modification.

Unlike the conventional HAMP program with the FHA HAMP program there are no imminent default components attached to it. The FHA-HAMP guidelines require that a borrower be past due at least one payment installment, due to a valid reason for a default. Homeowners are not be able to withhold their monthly repayments simply because they wish to qualify for modification assistance.

In addition to the non-imminent default eligibility requirements, part of the eligibility criteria to qualify for an FHA-HAMP modification, the homeowner must successfully participate in a four month trial modification period, rather than the three month trial modification period as is the requirement for the basic HAMP program.

If you have a loan that is insured or guaranteed by the Federal Housing Administration (FHA), you may be eligible for a program offered through them. Information on both the FHA and its participating servicers can be obtained through the FHA's National Servicing Center at (877) 622-8525.

USDA's Special Loan Servicing

If you have a loan that guaranteed by the United States Department of Agriculture's (USDA)Section 502 Single Family Housing Guaranteed Loan Program, you may be eligible for a program through that government agency. Contact your servicer for information.

Veteran's Administration Home Affordable Modification

If your loan is insured or guaranteed by the Department of Veterans Affairs (VA), you may be eligible for a program through that government agency.

For more information:

Call the V.A. Regional Loan Center at (877) 827-3702.

Visit HomeLoans.va.gov.

Home Affordable Foreclosure Alternatives Program

If a modification of any kind is not possible, and the homeowner need to move out of the home via a short sale, and if the mortgage qualifies, the Home Affordable Foreclosure Alternatives (HAFA) program is designed to provide relocation funds to assist with the moving expenses.

HAFA provides two options for transitioning out of your mortgage: a short sale or a Deed-in-Lieu (DIL) of foreclosure.

In a short sale, the mortgage company lets you sell your house for an amount that falls "short" of the amount you still owe.

In a DIL, the mortgage company lets you give the title back, transferring ownership back to them.

In either case, HAFA offers benefits that make the transition as favorable as possible:

- You can get free advice from HUD-approved housing counselors and licensed real estate professionals.

- Unlike conventional short sales, a HAFA short sale completely releases you from your mortgage debt after selling the property. This means you will no longer be responsible for the amount that falls "short" of the amount you still owe. The deficiency is guaranteed to be waived by the servicer.

- In a HAFA short sale, your mortgage company works with you to determine an acceptable sale price.

- HAFA has a less negative effect on your credit score than foreclosure or conventional short sales.
- When you close, HAFA may provide up to $10,000.00 in relocation assistance.

You may be eligible for HAFA if you meet all of the following criteria:

- You have a documented financial hardship.
- You have not purchased a new house within the last 12 months.
- Your first mortgage is less than $729,750.
- You obtained your mortgage on or before January 1, 2009.
- You must not have been convicted within the last 10 years of felony larceny, theft, fraud, forgery, money laundering or tax evasion in connection with a mortgage or real estate transaction.

HAFA is available for mortgages that are either owned or guaranteed by Fannie Mae and Freddie Mac or serviced by over 100 HAMP participating mortgage servicers. Contact your bank or mortgage lender to see if your mortgage is held by either Fannie Mae or Freddie Mac.

If you have already received an offer, be prepared to submit these additional forms:

- Alternative Request for Approval of Short Sale
- Executed sales contract

Treasury/FHA Second Lien Program

If you have a second mortgage and your first mortgage servicer participates in the FHA Short Refinance, you may be eligible to have your second mortgage on the same home reduced or eliminated through the FHA Second Lien Program.

If your second mortgage servicer agrees to participate, the total amount of your mortgage debt after the refinance cannot exceed 115 percent of your home's current value.

You may be eligible for FHA 2nd Lien Program if you meet the following criteria:

- You obtained your mortgage on or before January 1, 2009.
- There must have been no convictions within the last 10 years of felony larceny, theft, fraud, forgery, money laundering or tax evasion in connection with a mortgage or real estate transaction.
- If the servicer of your first mortgage agrees to an FHA Short Refinance and you have a second mortgage on the same home, the first mortgage servicer will work with the second mortgage servicer to reduce or eliminate the second mortgage.

More than a dozen mortgage servicers have agreed to review homeowners for FHA2LP when the first mortgage servicer has agreed to a refinance under FHA Short Refinance.

Home Affordable Refinance Program

If you are current on your mortgage payments and are not able to get traditional refinancing because the value of your home has dropped, you may be eligible to refinance through the Home Affordable Refinance Program (HARP).

HARP is designed to help you get a new, more affordable, more stable mortgage. HARP refinance loans require a loan application and underwriting process, and refinance fees will apply.

You may be eligible for HARP if you meet all of the following criteria:

- The mortgage must be owned or guaranteed by Freddie Mac or Fannie Mae.

- The mortgage must have been sold to Fannie Mae or Freddie Mac on or before May 31, 2009.

- The mortgage cannot have been refinanced under HARP previously, unless it is a Fannie Mae loan that was refinanced under HARP from March-May, 2009.

- The current loan-to-value (LTV) ratio must be greater than 80%.

- The borrower must be current on the mortgage at the time of the refinance, with a good payment history in the past 12 months.

Ask your mortgage servicer if they participate in HARP. Not all mortgage servicers do. Contact Fannie Mae or Freddie Mac for help in determining if you may be eligible for HARP.

Steps to refinance

There are just a few steps for you to follow in looking at this refinance opportunity:

- Determine whether your mortgage is owned or guaranteed by Fannie Mae or Freddie Mac by visiting their respective Loan Lookup Tools.

- Contact your current mortgage servicer to determine if Fannie Mae or Freddie Mac owns the mortgage, as well as inquiring about HARP.

- Compare rates and costs with additional mortgage companies to ensure best refinance terms.

- Visit Fannie Mae at KnowYourOptions.com or call (800)7Fannie.

- Look at the web site for Freddie Mac at www.FreddieMac.com the phone number is 1-800-Freddie.

This Program is set to end on December 31, 2016.

FHA Refinance for Homes with Negative Equity

If you are current on your mortgage payments but owe more than your home is worth, an FHA Short Refinance may be an option that your mortgage servicer could consider.

FHA Short Refinance is designed to help homeowners refinance into more affordable, more stable FHA-insured mortgage. If your current lender agrees to participate in this refinance, they will be required to reduce the amount you owe on your first mortgage to no more than 97.75 percent of your home's current value.

You may be eligible for FHA Short Refinance if you meet the following criteria:

- Your mortgage is not owned or guaranteed by Fannie Mae, Freddie Mac, FHA, VA or USDA.

- You owe more than your home is worth.

- You are current on your mortgage payments

- You occupy the house as your primary residence.

- You are eligible for the new loan under standard FHA underwriting requirements.

- Your total debt does not exceed 55 percent of your monthly gross income.

- You must not have been convicted within the last 10 years of felony, larceny, theft, fraud, forgery, money laundering, or tax evasion in connection with a mortgage or real estate transaction.

Participation:

- Participation of mortgage servicers is voluntary.
- Contact your mortgage servicer and ask whether they participate in FHA Short Refinance

If you have any questions about the FHA Short Refinance, contact the FHA National Servicing Center at (877) 622-8525

Home Affordable Unemployment Program (HAUP)

If you are unemployed and depending on your situation, MHA's Home Affordable Unemployment Program may reduce your mortgage payments to 31 percent of your income or suspend them altogether for 12 months or more.

You may be eligible for this program if you meet all of the following criteria:

- You are unemployed and eligible for unemployment benefits.
- You occupy the house as your primary residence.
- You have not previously received a HAMPSM modification.
- You obtained your mortgage on or before January 1, 2009.
- You owe up to $729,750 on your home.

Program Availability

There are over 100 HAMP-participating servicers who can offer HAUP to eligible unemployed homeowners.

- You may be required to make a partial payment, not to exceed 31 percent of your verified monthly gross (pre-tax) income including unemployment benefits.
- You will be evaluated for a HAMP mortgage modification at the end of your UP forbearance period if it is available at that time.

HAUP is not currently available for homeowners with mortgages held by Fannie Mae and Freddie Mac; as both of these servicers have their own forbearance arrangements for unemployed homeowners.

This program is set to expire on December 31, 2016.

Housing Finance Agency Innovation Fund for the Hardest Hit Housing Markets

Early in 2010, Treasury announced that the Hardest Hit Fund would provide more than $7.6 billion in aid for homeowners in 18 States, plus the District of Columbia, that were hit hardest by the economic crisis. These areas are:

Alabama • Arizona • California • Florida • Georgia • Illinois • Indiana Kentucky • Michigan • Mississippi • Nevada • New Jersey • North Carolina • Ohio • Oregon • Rhode Island • South Carolina • Tennessee Washington D.C.

Since 2010, State housing finance agencies have used the fund to develop programs that stabilize local housing markets and help families avoid foreclosure. Hardest Hit Fund programs complement the Making Home

Affordable Program but are not limited to homeowners eligible for Making Home Affordable.

Hardest Hit Fund programs vary state to state, but may include:

- Mortgage payment assistance for unemployed or underemployed homeowners
- Principal reduction to help homeowners get into more affordable mortgages
- Funding to eliminate homeowners' second lien loans
- Help for homeowners who are transitioning out of their homes and into more affordable places of residence.

Doing a Google search for your State's web page, then typing "Hardest Hit Fund" in that web page should also direct you towards the State housing finance agency.

What Does the Lender Modification Program have to Offer?

If a HAMP modification is not possible, what alternatives are there; what modification programs do the banks and lenders have to offer?

Let's take a look at what the MHA offers, as a way of setting the stage for the bank/lender modifications.

Some of the modification programs that the MHA offers allow for a permanent reduction of the interest rate, rather than a step rate reduction. This has the advantage to the homeowner of their never having to worry about their rate increasing. The other advantage is that some of the newer MHA modifications do not have any three-month trial period in them; there is an automatic permanent modification set up upon approval of the modification.

Not all investors will take part in the MHA, so the only alternative would be to have the in-house modification done.

However, this is not without its shortfalls too. We'll go into some detail in this chapter.

Most of the lenders will have a guideline, sometimes known as a "waterfall", which they will have to follow as part of the modification process. This waterfall is separate from the requirement to process all eligible mortgages for HAMP either first, or concurrently.

Assuming that your mortgage is not eligible for HAMP assistance, perhaps because your mortgage lender does not participate in this program, lenders will try to solve your mortgage problems in the following order:

Mortgage Repayment Plans

Depending on the amount of payments past due, as well as verification of your gross income and expenses, using 31% payment to income ratio, your lender may simply get you caught up with your payments by spreading the delinquent payments over a set period of time, usually between 3-6 months. Some lenders will spread the repayment plans over a 12 month period, but these are becoming the exception and not the rule. While this plan does forestall any possible default/foreclosure action from being taken, it will have a continued impact on your credit score, as the scores are based upon your contractual payments. The arrears will continue to be reported as missing until the repayment plan is completed.

Principal Forbearance Plan

There may be times when the homeowner may have a temporary problem meeting their mortgage payments, e.g., un-planned medical or automobile expense for example, and, while they can normally afford the mortgage payments, need some breathing room for a short time in order to deal with this unplanned expense. The length of time for the forbearance is generally going to be for 3 months.

When your lender works out a principle forbearance plan, your monthly repayment may be reduced by 30-40, or, in some cases the repayment amount can be reduced up to 100 percent.

Your eligibility for this program, as well as the percentage of the payment reduction, will be based on your total household income, so you may be asked to provide proof of income at this point

Now, depending on your lender, they may or may not continue to file an active credit report on your mortgage payments during this forbearance period.

Rather than report your mortgage as being either paid or unpaid, your credit report will read "Unknown".

This is a neutral reporting score, and, while your credit score will be affected, the effects will not be as severe as it would have been had they reported the payments as "unpaid".

At the end of the forbearance period, it will be expected for you to repay the missed payments, in addition to the regular monthly repayment that is due.

Failure to do this can result in your forbearance plan being placed in default, and your credit score amended to reflect 90 days delinquency.

In-House/Proprietary Mortgage Modification

If it is determined that neither of the above two options will work, the lender will begin to review your file for a possible Loan Modification. At this point, they will be reviewing the documentation you have provided to them, to see what solutions are suitable for you.

The majority of the home modification requests that I've read have requested that we would either reduce the principle outstanding balance borrowed, and/or reduce the interest rate to a flat 2%, as well as write off the delinquent balances outstanding.

As mentioned earlier, modifications are done so that the homeowner's monthly repayment, and /or interest rates can be adjusted in line with the current income levels, in order to make those mortgage payments more affordable. There's usually no change to the maturity date of the mortgage, nor would there usually would not be any write off of past due amounts, nor a reduction of outstanding principle balance; although this has been known to happen on the odd occasion, and then only under specific investor approval. This is the exception and not the rule.

In some cases, under HAMP guidelines a modification will occur in which some form of principle reduction would take place, but this is not a regular occurrence and should not be counted on.

We also need to keep in mind, as has been noted earlier, that the terms of modification are set either by the lender themselves, or, if the mortgage is serviced for a third party investor, by that investor directly.

Within the modification process there are several component steps that will usually be followed. The first process that will be tried is known, by some lenders, as a "Capitalization Modification". After reviewing your income and expenses, and determining that your gross income falls within the 31-42% payment to income ratio, your underwriter will try to see if they can place your payment delinquency on top of the outstanding principle balance. This will effectively bring your account current and up to date. At this point in the modification process, your interest rates will not be changed.

What will change will be the monthly repayments. Another alternative to this process is when the underwriter will then take your delinquent balance and place it at the end of the mortgage. The interest rate will not change, nor will the monthly repayments. What will change will be the delinquency, your account will be considered current and up-to-date.

In the event that this Rate Capitalization review doesn't work, the underwriter will then see if a modification can be achieved by both placing your delinquency at the end of the mortgage, in an interest free balloon period for up to 480 months, as well as doing a reduction of your interest rate on a quarter of a percent basis, until your modified repayment falls within the 31-42% threshold. I have done many of these where we reduced the interest rate to the floor rate of 2%.

Once this rate reduction has been achieved, the investor may allow for a permanent reduction of the interest rate. More times than not the policy guidelines will only allow for something that is known as a "Step Rate Reduction". This simply means that modified interest rate will be reduced for a period of time, anywhere from two to five years. On the fifth year, the rate will increase by one percent, and will continue to increase by a percent a year, until that interest rate hits the Freddie Mac interest rate that was recorded at the original time of the application.

For example, if the Freddie Mac interest rate at the time of the review for a loan modification was 4.75%; your interest rate will never go higher than that amount at the end of two to five year step rate period.

In some cases, notably with the HAMP type modifications, the mortgage modification will produce a permanent interest rate reduction that does away with the step rate process altogether. I've been able to bring interest rates down from 9.5 % to 2% for the life of the loan, regardless of what kind of mortgage, e.g., interest rate only, ARM, or principle, interest and insurance, the homeowner has.

These permanent interest rate reductions are still the exception and not the rule, however and are decided on a case by case basis.

In any event, even a step rate reduction for a period of five years, and then having it cap out at a lower interest rate will still, in most instances, save the homeowner money over all.

Keep in mind that while the reduction in interest rate will generally tend to bring about a reduction of repayments, the outstanding delinquency is still out there and will need to be addressed at some point prior to the maturity date of the mortgage. There is a caveat to this however.

If your mortgage is not one that has principle interest, taxes and insurances (PITI), and is either an ARM, or some form of interest only mortgage, the modification will generally not bring about any sizable reduction of repayment, as the principle balance outstanding will not have been hugely affected, and any arrears on the account will only increase the outstanding interest payments.

It's a catch twenty-two situation. The only good side to this is that any modification offered will only be done so if the homeowner is able to afford it under the payment to income ratio criteria.

The expectation is that, at some point, during the next three to five years, of the modification, the housing market will right itself up to the point where the home is worth what it should be, thus allowing you, the homeowner the opportunity to do a refinance, wrap the balloon payment into a new principle, and, hopefully, get better terms and conditions on your mortgage payments.

SHORT SALE

There are times when no matter what, a loan modification is just not possible. This may be due to the outstanding balance being so great that the mortgage would have to be rewritten beyond the 31% mark. Another reason may be that the total gross income in the household is simply not enough to maintain any sort of mortgage repayments.

In some cases, the investor may not allow for either a reduction of interest, participation in HAMP or with any sort of modification, beyond a repayment or a forbearance plan. This restriction is typically attached to a particular sub-prime mortgage, where, in the eyes of the investor, it is simply less expensive, and less risky in the long run, to cut their losses, and either take the property back for rental purposes, or allow it to be sold off via short sale, deed in lieu, or straight foreclosure.

Once the decision is made that modification assistance is not possible, the discussion is guided away from home retention, to that of debt reduction.

There are other options available to the home owner, and are confined to either: bringing the delinquent account current, doing a voluntary surrender of the property, known as a Deed in Lieu, Short Sale, or letting the property go into Foreclosure.

Of the four options, Short Sale is generally considered to be the better option, if only because it will actually reduce the balance outstanding, afford the homeowner some measure of relief as their commitment to the property is ended quicker than it would be otherwise, and their financial obligations to the home, are generally severed with the sale.

A short sale is a sale of real estate in which the house is sold for the current fair market value, which is less than the outstanding principle balance owed on the mortgage.

Once the sale takes place, the lien holder (lender) will release any claim on the debt and accept the reduced balances. Any balance shortfall is known as a deficiency balance and will still be owed to the lender, unless a prior agreement is made. Usually this outstanding balance is reported to the Internal Revenue Service on a form known as a 1099-C.

The 1099c will report that outstanding balance as untaxed income and the I.R.S. may seek to collect taxes on this.

But what about the banks and lenders? Will they attempt to recover the remainder of the unpaid principle balance?

This depends on where the property is located, as there are several States in the country, which classified as "Non-Recoverable" States, which means that outstanding debt cannot be recovered from the former homeowner.

California for example, and in certain other States, legislation was passed to preclude deficiencies after a short sale is approved. The same is true of lenders on first loans and lenders on second loans — once the short sale is approved; no deficiencies are permitted after the short sale. (In the State of California, the applicable law is SB 931, SB 458 - Calif. Code of Civil Procedure §580e).

There is a chart in the Appendix of the book that lists which States are recoverable and which are not.

A short sale is also seen as a better alternative to foreclosure because it mitigates additional fees and costs to both the creditor and borrower.

While both the short sale and the deed in lieu will result in a negative credit report on the property owner, the negative reporting on a short sale, when compared to a foreclosure, is far less damaging, and will not remain on the credit report as long as a foreclosure will.

In addition to the Treasury's HAFA program, some lenders also have a relocation assistance program, and can offer amounts of between $3,000-$10.000.00 to assist in relocation funding to the homeowner.

Like the HAFA program, the lenders will not release any relocation funds until the on completion of the Short Sale Process.

There are a few reasons why lenders will offer such assistance for relocation on a short sale. They want to make the property transition as painless as possible by assisting the homeowner with moving or lease deposit expenses. There have been times where I have released funds between $2000.00 and $6000.00.

The other reason for lenders to offer this financial assistance is to push the process away from a foreclosure, which is a lose-lose proposition for both the homeowner and the lender. The homeowner will end up with a stain on their credit records that will be listed for a minimum of five years, and while they may be able to apply for credit within 24 months, the rate of interest offered to them will usually be at a premium due to the foreclosure. For the lender, a foreclosure means legal bills, a process that can take over a year to complete; in the meantime, there is no income coming in from that property.

Relocation assistance is not automatic, and is offered as a courtesy, and funds are not be issued until after the sales contracts have been signed, returned to the lender, and filed with the proper County authorities.

There are tax consequences with the relocation assistance, as any financial assistance would be subject to being taxed. An IRS form W9 will be sent out to the homeowner which would need to be filled out and returned to the lender along with the short sale documentation.

A short sale is not the same as a regular property sale, so don't expect to get any money back for yourself from the sale.

How Does a Short Sale Get Started in the first place?

So, how do you get a short sale started in the first place? When should a short sale be considered?

Let's answer the last question first.

While a short sale can be considered at any time by the homeowner, even before applying for any modification assistance, they will have to get in contact with their lender to see if they will allow the process to go forward.

In the event that a short sale is allowable, this will provide some much needed relief to homeowners, who worn down by the struggle of trying to maintain their monthly mortgage payments.

I have had many conversations with homeowners from all over the country who, rather than proceed with a loan modification, made the decision to go directly to the short sale route. Some of these homeowners were using this particular property as a non-owner occupied property. It was rental property for example, so they did not have as much of an emotional attachment to the house. But this was, in my experience, the exception and not the rule.

Once the decision to move forward with a short sale, the phone call is placed to me, and then, after some discussion with the homeowner, I will tell him/her how the process will work.

There are two things that the homeowner must do before considering a short sale:

- First: Get qualified tax/legal advice to see what, if any, tax liabilities you may have because of a possible 1099c being issued And

- Second: Get a licensed real estate agent/realtor or broker who is not only familiar with the short sale process, but who is familiar with how the process works for your particular lender. No two lenders will require the same information, and you may end up sending either more paperwork than is needed, or not sending enough. If the latter happens, this will tend to halt progress on any short sale action until that paperwork is submitted.

While we are on the subject of real estate agents, you need to feel 100% confident in their ability to both do the job properly, and that they will have someone in place to assist them with the process.

Phone calls or contact via computer will need to be done on a regular basis, and some realtors, despite all the best intentions, may not always follow through as often as they should. The better organized real estate agents will have tend to have an assistant who will make that regular contact with the lender.

What paperwork is asked for to begin the short sale process?

While the following requirements may be generalized, they are, for the most part, applicable across the board with whatever lender you may be working with.

Realtor:

- Letter of Authorization (signed and dated by seller) Letter to include names of each individual who will be calling on your behalf.
- HUD-1
- Copy of the MLS Listing
- Copy of Listing Contract
- Copy of Purchase Contract (if applicable)
- Review Hardship letter /Opt Out letter stating that seller does not wish to pursue any further modification/HAMP alternatives

Seller:

- IRS 1040 Tax returns, for the past two years' with all schedules and attachments, as well as most recent W'2s
- If Self-employed, either Year to Date, or most recent quarters signed and dated Profit and Loss Statement.
- Three month's bank statements
- Current monthly budget
- All mortgages with account numbers (if applicable)
- If you have a discharged bankruptcy, a copy of the Court issued Certificate of Discharge will be required.

If there has been a bankruptcy involved, then there will need to be a letter of authorization from your bankruptcy attorney, which will allow the lender to speak with you and the realtor. (*Please Note: If there is current bankruptcy involved, before the short sale can be finalized, the bankruptcy court will have to approve the final disposition of the sale. It is highly suggested that legal counsel be sought before, during, and after the short sale process.)*

- Hardship letter /Opt Out letter stating that you do not wish to pursue any further modification/HAMP alternatives.
- Last 30 day's pay stubs (if applicable)

It needs to be pointed out, again, that these requirements are only meant for general informational purposes, and that you may not need all of the above material for submission for short sale review.

After the paperwork has been submitted and a buyer has submitted their proposal for purchase, it's a matter of the homeowner waiting for the approval for the investor. Generally this can take anywhere from one to three months, if that long.

If there are additional forced liens against the property, those other lien holders will have to give their consent for the short sale, as they will also have to be paid off. However, the process of short sale generally tends to come as a result of there NOT being any mortgage modification alternatives, and that the short sale is being done to avoid foreclosure. Faced with this reality, most lenders who hold liens on the property will tend to settle for a reduced payout. Remember that 10-20 % of something is a lot better than the 100% of nothing, should the property become foreclosed.

One final thing for you to consider while you do a short sale; while many lenders will have an "arms-length" clause built in, e.g., you can't get wife, uncle, mom, dad, brother, or other close relative to buy the property on a reduced short sale basis, there are lenders who do make allowances for this. This makes sense to me, as the property is disposed of at the fair market value. The home is not at risk for being vacant for an indeterminate period of time, and the homeowner can remain the house. It would not hurt to have your realtor make inquiries on your behalf concerning this policy.

Deed in Lieu of Foreclosure

It may not always be possible to get a prospective buyer for the property due to many circumstances, including the price of the house.

If the property has been on the marked for a prolonged period of time, and there has either not been any interest in the house, or if the purchase offers being submitted to your lender are being rejected due to the bid being too low, and if all counter offers are being rejected, what happens next?

The only other non-foreclosure alternative is by a voluntary surrender of the property via a deed in lieu of foreclosure. You are, in effect telling your lender that you have done everything possible to resolve the delinquency either by modification of the mortgage or by the short sale process, but have not been able to do so.

So, when can you apply for a deed in lieu of foreclosure? It really depends upon the lender. Some lenders will not make allowances for any sort of reduced price sale. Other lenders may require that the property have gone through the short sale process for a minimum of 90 consecutive days. Other lenders do not have any such restrictions.

When speaking with homeowners about the deed in lieu, I told them one important thing: "Depending on the laws of the State where you live, you will need to get qualified legal/tax advice as there may be taxation consequence as a result of the ultimate dispersal of the property, due to our having to send out a 1099c form."

What, if any, tax consequences are there by you doing a deed in lieu of foreclosure?

Some potential consequences of a deed in lieu are that if the house is classified as being a non-owner occupied residence (if it is not a primary residence), you may be required to pay taxes on the deficiency amount, which is that difference between what the current outstanding balance is on the mortgage and the value of the property.

However, you may not actually have to worry about any tax liabilities. The United States Federal Government placed into law something known as The Mortgage Forgiveness Debt Relief Act of 2007 (IRS), which addresses the issue of the tax implications of a deed in lieu of foreclosure.

According to their web site, "The Mortgage Debt Relief Act of 2007 generally allows taxpayers to exclude income from the discharge of debt on their principal residence. Debt reduced through mortgage restructuring, as well as mortgage debt forgiven in connection with a foreclosure, qualifies for the relief."

The Debt Relief Act of 2007 was only originally meant to last until the end of 2010, but was extended through the Emergency Economic Stabilization Act of 2008 to the end of 2012. The 2007 Act was extended again, as a result of the fiscal cliff legislation early in 2013 and has since been extended until the end of 2016. As of the date of this writing, there is no indication as to whether or not the 2007 act will be extended for another year.

What does the Mortgage Forgiveness Debt Relief Act of 2007 actually mean for the tax payer who is in the situation of having to deal with a deed in lieu of foreclosure or a foreclosure itself? Simply put, it means that if all or part of the mortgage debt on your principal residence is forgiven in any tax year from 2007 to 2013, you might be able to exclude as much as $2 million of that forgiven debt from your taxable income. Or in other words, there are no 1099c consequences.

As of now, 2013, the act provides that you do not have to pay federal taxes on the deficiency amount if:

- The deed in lieu of foreclosure is for your primary residence;
- The original loan was used to purchase, build or improve the primary residence; and
- The original loan is secured by your primary residence.

You may be able to avoid potential tax liabilities if you are insolvent (have more debt than assets) at the time the deed in lieu of foreclosure was facilitated; and you filed for bankruptcy prior to the closing on your home.

So, you've returned the keys, and have dealt with your 1099c worries. What next?

What about your credit score? Well, the bad news is that your score will have an adverse impact on it, as your file will be listed as being in a permanent default state. However, the impact on your credit score will not be as severe or as long lasting as it would be if the property had gone into the foreclosure stage, as we will see in the next chapter

FORECLOSURE

The foreclosure process is the act of last resort, due to the long lasting and public damage that it can cost to the homeowner.

The damage to a credit report can be long lasting, anywhere from 2-7 years, depending on which credit bureau is reporting your debt.

While it is true that within 24 months you should be able to apply for new credit, from a risk assessment/underwriting perspective, you would be classified as a high risk customer. As a result of this, you probably will not be given the best interest repayment options.

Depending on which part of the country you live in, you could also find yourself ending up in to court by the lender for the outstanding balance, even though you walked away from the property. The added expense of court fees, etc., should make the foreclosure rather problematic.

It is true that not all foreclosures are "recoverable"; in some parts of the United States, California, for example, are non-recoverable; that is to say, once you leave the home due to foreclosure, you no longer have any liability to that debt. The lender has ownership of the home and that's all that they're entitled to.

At the end of this book, there is a map of the United States, which is accurate at the time of this writing, of all fifty states and what their foreclosure procedures are.

Even if there is no risk of any recoverable action being taken against you, there are at least three potential liabilities that can affect you: credit liability, deficiency liability, and income tax liabilities as a result of entering into a foreclosure.

It's important to be aware of your own personal circumstances and the potential effects that these liabilities can have on you and your household.

It is important to remember that any sort of default on your mortgage agreement will have a negative impact on your credit, and while this may not be important at this time, I cannot emphasize enough that, going forward in 2-3 years, it may be of some importance as you begin the rebuilding process of your credit.

One reason the foreclosure is considered to be the "third rail" on the track is that the process is a matter of public record. Credit agencies will have this reported, and it can remain on your file for up to seven years. This will have a rather severe impact on your ability to gain decent credit. The only possible exception to this circumstance might be if the foreclosure resulted in losing the property due to natural disaster, loss of employment, or by serious illness. Federal law does provide you with the right to file an explanation with the credit report; but only if there was an extenuating circumstance which caused the foreclosure.

A deficiency liability will occur when the foreclosed property sells for an amount which is less than the current outstanding balance, which will more than likely be the case.

For example: If the outstanding balance is $350.000.00, and the sale amount is $295.000.00, the balance remaining, or the deficiency balance, will be $55.000.00, this is the balance that the borrower may be liable for.

However, due to a set of complex legal and accounting reasons, deficiency balances are rare in foreclosures, and it would be difficult to have any such liability enforced against the borrower. For example, in California, the process that most lenders will follow, if they elect to bid at the foreclosure sale on their own loan, is that they will "credit bid" total, or nearly total all of the loan balance, regardless of the actual value of the property. The reason being, of course, that they want to recoup as much of the outstanding balance as possible. Frankly, they will have a better chance doing it this way than by pursuing the borrower. As mentioned earlier, California is one of a handful of States that has what is known as "anti-deficiency" protection, in the form of Code of Civil Procedure 550d, which prevents the lender from obtaining a deficiency after the foreclosure of a residential property under a deed of trust. As most of the foreclosures of residential property in the State of California happen under a deed of trust and not under a judicial foreclosure, there would not be any liability for any deficiency.

Finally, let's take a look at what, more likely than not, will affect you.

While a foreclosure sale may relieve you of your financial commitment to the lender, there is the likelihood that you will have to deal with the Internal Revenue Service at some point. While tax laws are complex and are subject to interpretation, there are some general principles that are fairly certain to affect you.

The IRS will treat the foreclosure as a regular sale, and a 1099c for the amount that was bid on the sale will be issued.

As with any sort of sale, there could be a tax liability if there were any sort of gain from the sale. For purposes of clarification you may need to have; "gain" from a prior sale is where you rolled over the "gain" from the sale of your previous residence to the one that is now being foreclosed on. Another possibility would be if you refinanced your house, took cash out, or if you had a HELOC (Home Equity Line of Credit), or a second deed of trust where there was an outstanding balance.

Keep in mind, however, that both The Mortgage Forgiveness and Debt Relief Acts of 2007 do provide former homeowners with limited tax relief following a foreclosure. If you lost your home to foreclosure between 2007 and 2012, you are not liable for any taxes that may result from the forgiven debt, as long as you report the debt properly when you file your taxes. With the extension given in January 2013, this protection should continue through the remainder of 2013. There is no indication at the time of this writing that the 2007 Act will be extended for a further year.

In any event, you must fill out Form 982 notifying the IRS that you are claiming your tax protection under the Mortgage Forgiveness and Debt Relief Act. Attach Form 982 to your tax return before you file your annual taxes.

There is one more thing to remember about the Mortgage Forgiveness and Debt Relief Act and the foreclosure process: not every homeowner who is involved with a foreclosure will be protected by this Act. If the property is not owner occupied, e.g., it is either a vacation home, or an investment property, or if you are able to provide proof that you've lived in the property for at least a portion of the year prior to the foreclosure of the property, you may be able to claim at least partial tax protection that is in proportion to the months of the year that you actually resided in the property. Tax protection for individuals will cap out at one million dollars. Or, in other words, you must pay taxes on any amount your lender forgives in excess of one million dollars. For married couples, the amount is two million dollars.

Keep in mind also that if tax protection provisions are not available for you, then you would need to make immediate arrangements with the IRS to repay the balances owed. The IRS does have the right to garnish any tax refunds that would normally be sent to you in the future, as well as the placement of a tax lien on any additional property that you may own.

Now these tax rules are complex and should not be overlooked or treated lightly. As has been mentioned earlier:

Many people will tend to overlook this part of the foreclosure process, only to find that they still have some tax responsibility for a home that they no longer own due to foreclosure or for the deed in lieu which was written earlier in this book.

Bankruptcy

Let's now look at what many would consider an action of last resort Bankruptcy.

There are two main types of consumer bankruptcy that are typically found in the modification process, Chapter 7 and Chapter 13.

A Chapter 7 bankruptcy is known as a "liquidation" bankruptcy, in that most of your assets are liable to be remanded to the bankruptcy trustee on behalf of your creditors.

A Chapter 13 bankruptcy is more akin to a payment plan you work out with the bankruptcy court to pay back your debts over a three- to five-year period. If you have a home of any significant value and you file Chapter 7, you are liable to lose the home to the bankruptcy trustee. If you can afford a payment plan as structured in a Chapter 13 bankruptcy, you will likely be able to keep your home.

Reaffirmation

If you want to keep your home when you file bankruptcy, you must file a reaffirmation agreement with the court. Essentially, a reaffirmation agreement states that you agree to the liability of your current mortgage, regardless of the outcome of your bankruptcy proceedings. In other words, you simply keep making the payments on your house as if you had never filed for bankruptcy and hold on to your home. A reaffirmation agreement is effective only if you are current on your mortgage. After signing a reaffirmation, you cannot claim your mortgage debt as being discharged in bankruptcy.

Equity in Home

If you have limited equity in your home, you can still file a Chapter 7, along with a reaffirmation agreement, and possibly keep your home. California allows you to exempt up to $75,000 of equity in your home if you are single or $100,000 if you are married, even in a Chapter 7 bankruptcy. If you are underwater on your mortgage or have limited equity, you may be able to exempt that equity in a Chapter 7 proceeding and reaffirm your mortgage.

State Laws and Guidelines

The state in which you file bankruptcy can play a large role in how your home is handled. While bankruptcy is a federal procedure, each state determines its own exemption levels, and some states are more generous than others. For example, while California's homestead exemption runs up to $100,000 as of 2010, some states may allow you to keep homes of any value in a bankruptcy proceeding.

Foreclosure

If you are underwater on your mortgage, you can simply file Chapter 7 bankruptcy, stop making payments and walk away from your mortgage. This is true in all states, including California. Assuming you qualify for bankruptcy, you will lose your house in this scenario, but you will also no longer be liable for the mortgage debt

STATE FORECLOSURE PROCEDURES

The HUD web site has the following information concerning foreclosures that bear repeating at this time:

> *Foreclosure processes are different in every state. If you are worried about making your mortgage payments, then you should learn about your state's foreclosure laws and processes. Differences among states range from the notices that must be posted or mailed, redemption periods, and the scheduling and notices issued regarding the auctioning of the property. However, a general understanding of what to expect can be found on our foreclosure timeline.*

In general, mortgage companies start foreclosure processes about 3-6 months after the first missed mortgage payment. Late fees are charged after 10-15 days; however, most mortgage companies recognize that homeowners may be facing short-term financial hardships. It is extremely important that you stay in contact with your lender within the first month after missing a payment.

After 30 days, the borrower is in default, and the foreclosure processes begin to accelerate. If you do not call the bank and ignore the calls of your lender, then the foreclosure process will begin much earlier. At any time during the process, talk to your lender or a housing counselor about the different alternatives and solutions that may exist.

Three types of foreclosures may be initiated at this time: judicial, power of sale and strict foreclosure. All types of foreclosure require public notices to be issued and all parties to be notified regarding the proceedings. Once properties are sold through an auction, families have a small amount of time to find a new place to live and move out before the sheriff issues an eviction.

Judicial Foreclosure All states allow this type of foreclosure, and some require it. The lender files suit with the judicial system, and the borrower will receive a note in the mail demanding payment. The borrower then has only 30 days to respond with a payment in order to avoid foreclosure. If a payment is not made after a certain time period, the mortgage property is then sold through an auction to the highest bidder, carried out by a local court or sheriff's office.

Power of Sale This type of foreclosure, also known as statutory foreclosure, is allowed by many states if the mortgage includes a power of sale clause. After a homeowner has defaulted on mortgage payments, the lender sends out notices demanding payments. Once an established waiting period has passed, the mortgage company, rather than local courts or sheriff's office, carries out a public auction. Non-judicial foreclosure auctions are often more expedient, though they may be subject to judicial review to ensure the legality of the proceedings.

Strict Foreclosure A small number of states allow this type of foreclosure. In strict foreclosure proceedings, the lender files a lawsuit on the homeowner that has defaulted. If the borrower cannot pay the mortgage within a specific timeline ordered by the court, the property goes directly back to the mortgage holder. Generally, strict foreclosures take place only when the debt amount is greater than the value of the property.

JUDICIAL AND NON JUDICAL STATES

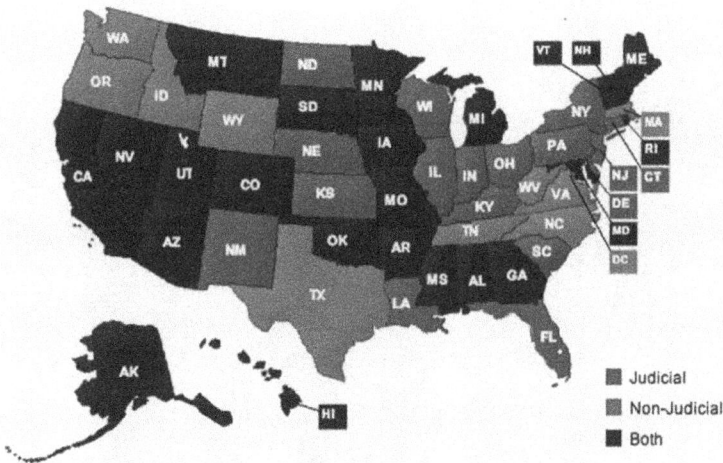

JUDICAL	NON JUDICIAL
Use state court system during foreclosure	Use trustee to process foreclosure; courts not required
Homeowner carries the deed	Beneficiary (investor) carries the deed
Default recorded at county courthouse	Default recorded at county courthouse
Bank Investor must go through courts before foreclosure process can be initiated	Bank Investor does not have to go through courts to initiate foreclosure process
Court verifies default status; sends homeowner Notice of Default	No Notice of Default required; may send Notice of Trustee Sale notification
In most states, homeowner has 60 days at this stage in the process before home is sold at public auction	In most states, homeowner has 22-30 days at this stage in the process before home is sold at public auction

AVERAGE NUMBER OF DAYS FOR
FORECLOSURE PROCESS COMPLETION

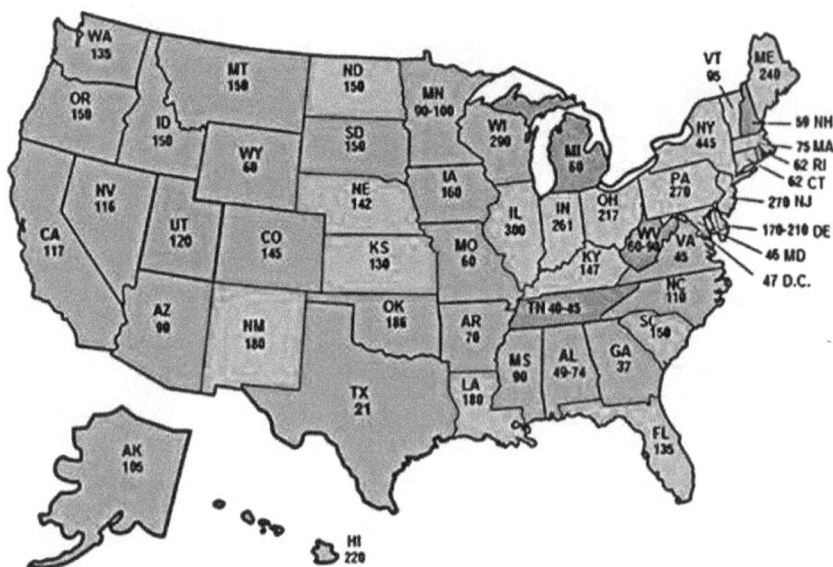

WA 135
OR 150
MT 150
ID 150
WY 60
ND 150
SD 150
MN 90-100
WI 290
MI 60
NV 116
UT 120
CO 145
NE 142
IA 160
IL 300
IN 261
OH 217
CA 117
AZ 90
NM 180
KS 130
MO 60
KY 147
WV 60-90
VA 45
OK 186
AR 70
TN 40-85
NC 110
SC 150
MS 90
AL 49-74
GA 37
TX 21
LA 180
FL 135
AK 105
HI 220
VT 95
ME 240
NY 445
PA 270
50 NH
75 MA
62 RI
62 CT
270 NJ
170-210 DE
46 MD
47 D.C.

SOME FINAL THOUGHTS

It is hoped that this book will have empowered you with a better sense of what the process is and what the actual requirements are for loan modifications, and that with this understanding, you will have a better idea of which direction is best for you and your family.

We've taken a look at some of the main components to home loan modifications, for both the Federal Government, in the form of the Home Affordable Modification Program (HAMP) has to offer to distressed homeowners, as well as some of the potential programs that the banks and other lenders may have to offer qualified homeowners.

As I earlier wrote, one of the biggest problems that I encountered during my time as a Modification Specialist, was the lack of knowledge that a good number of my customers had concerning the modification process either because they were perhaps relying on information given to them from someone who had a friend whose friend had a modification, or by their 3rd party advocate who did not explain the process clearly enough to them, or that.

To me this is the most damaging thing of all. After all, Mr. and Mrs. Smith are paying the law firm of Dewey, Cheatum & Howe retainer fees of up to $8000.00 so that the homeowner can let someone else do the leg work. Having spent so much money, and not getting an accurate picture of what the process is, is bad enough, but when that homeowner is having a struggle to get ten cents out of two nickels, and has sunk in so much money for so little return, it does tend to make my blood boil.

This mortgage modification crisis is not showing any signs of slowing down any time soon. More and more and more distressed homeowners are seeking help from both their lenders and from the Federal Government. While the lending institutions and the Federal Government are working at bring these problems under control, it will take time.

It is hoped that the knowledge of how the process works will make the waiting time for your modification to be a bit less stressful. It is sincerely hoped this book will have helped in your understanding of how the modification process works, as well as what your options can be.

REFERENCE MATERIAL, GLOSSARY OF TERMS, LENDERS DIRECTORY OF HAMP PARTICIPANTS

Here are some examples of the various forms that may be required of you to submit to the banks, as well as examples of Profit and Loss Statements that are required in some instances from those who are self-employed.

In addition a glossary of terms and a directory of lenders and banking institutions who, as of this publication date (2015) participate in the Hamp/Making Home Affordable Program.

BOBS LAWN AND GARDEN CARE
PROFIT AND LOSS STATEMENT
MARCH 31ST 2012 THROUGH APRIL 30TH 2013

Ordinary Income/Expense
Income

Landscaping Services	57,860.36
Markup Income	815.00
Retail Sales	383.03
Service	6,640.00
Total Income	65,698.39

Cost of Goods Sold

Cost of Goods Sold	4,220.25
Total COGS	4,220.25
Gross Profit	61,478.14

Expense

Payroll Expenses	37,820.65
Automobile	738.05
Bank Service Charges	73.50
Delivery Fee	15.00
Insurance	1,835.00
Interest Expense	470.91
Job Expenses	2,427.25
Mileage Reimbursement	0.00
Professional Fees	375.00
Rent	2,400.00
Repairs	45.00
Tools and Misc. Equipment	735.00
Uncategorized Expenses	0.00
Utilities	655.55
Total Expense	47,590.91
Net Ordinary Income	13,887.23

Other Income/Expense
Other Income

Misc Income	762.50
Interest Income	91.11
Total Other Income	853.61
Net Other Income	853.61
Net Income	14,740.84

Household Budget Expenses	
Mortgage	
2nd Mortgage – HELOC	
Homeowners Insurance	
Property Tax	
City Utilities, trash, sewer, etc.	
Gas – Electric	
Phone-Internet-Cable	
Food	
Gasoline - Car Expenses	
Life Insurance	
Health Insurance	
Medical Expenses	
Credit Card Payments	
Credit Card Payments	
Credit Card Payments	
Credit Card Payments	
Store Card Payments	
Automobile Loan	
Unsecured Personal Loan	
Dry Cleaning -Business Related	
Monthly Parking-Business Related	

Name: _____ Date: _____

Name: _____ Date: _____

Form **4506T-EZ**	**Short Form Request for Individual Tax Return Transcript**	
(Rev. January 2010)		OMB No. 1545-2154
Department of the Treasury Internal Revenue Service	▶ Request may not be processed if the form is incomplete or illegible.	

Tip. Use Form 4506T-EZ to order a 1040 series tax return transcript free of charge.

1a Name shown on tax return. If a joint return, enter the name shown first.	**1b First social security number on tax return**
2a If a joint return, enter spouse's name shown on tax return.	**2b Second social security number if joint tax return**

3 Current name, address (including apt., room, or suite no.), city, state, and ZIP code

4 Previous address shown on the last return filed if different from line 3

5 If the transcript is to be mailed to a third party (such as a mortgage company), enter the third party's name, address, and telephone number. The IRS has no control over what the third party does with the tax information.

Third party name	Telephone number

Address (including apt., room, or suite no.), city, state, and ZIP code

6 **Year(s) requested.** Enter the year(s) of the return transcript you are requesting (for example, "2008"). Most requests will be processed within 10 business days.

_____ _____ _____ _____

Caution. If the transcript is being mailed to a third party, ensure that you have filled in line 6 before signing. Sign and date the form once you have filled in line 6. Completing these steps helps to protect your privacy.

Note. If the IRS is unable to locate a return that matches the taxpayer identity information provided above, or if IRS records indicate that the return has not been filed, the IRS may notify you or the third party that it was unable to locate a return, or that a return was not filed, whichever is applicable.

Signature of taxpayer(s). I declare that I am the taxpayer whose name is shown on either line 1a or 2a. If the request applies to a joint return, **either** husband or wife must sign. **Note.** For transcripts being sent to a third party, this form must be received within 120 days of signature date.

		Telephone number of taxpayer on line 1a or 2a
Sign Here	▶ Signature (see instructions)	Date
	▶ Spouse's signature	Date

For Privacy Act and Paperwork Reduction Act Notice, see page 2.   Cat. No. 54185S   Form **4506T-EZ** (Rev. 01-2010)

Form **4506-T**	**Request for Transcript of Tax Return**	
(Rev. January 2010)	▶ Request may be rejected if the form is incomplete or illegible.	OMB No. 1545-1872
Department of the Treasury Internal Revenue Service		

Tip. Use Form 4506-T to order a transcript or other return information free of charge. See the product list below. You can also call 1-800-829-1040 to order a transcript. If you need a copy of your return, use **Form 4506, Request for Copy of Tax Return.** There is a fee to get a copy of your return.

1a Name shown on tax return. If a joint return, enter the name shown first.	1b First social security number on tax return or employer identification number (see instructions)
2a If a joint return, enter spouse's name shown on tax return.	2b Second social security number if joint tax return

3 Current name, address (including apt., room, or suite no.), city, state, and ZIP code

4 Previous address shown on the last return filed if different from line 3

5 If the transcript or tax information is to be mailed to a third party (such as a mortgage company), enter the third party's name, address, and telephone number. The IRS has no control over what the third party does with the tax information.

Caution. *If the transcript is being mailed to a third party, ensure that you have filled in line 6 and line 9 before signing. Sign and date the form once you have filled in these lines. Completing these steps helps to protect your privacy.*

6   **Transcript requested.** Enter the tax form number here (1040, 1065, 1120, etc.) and check the appropriate box below. Enter only one tax form number per request. ▶ _____

a   **Return Transcript,** which includes most of the line items of a tax return as filed with the IRS. A tax return transcript does not reflect changes made to the account after the return is processed. Transcripts are only available for the following returns: Form 1040 series, Form 1065, Form 1120, Form 1120A, Form 1120H, Form 1120L, and Form 1120S. Return transcripts are available for the current year and returns processed during the prior 3 processing years. Most requests will be processed within 10 business days . . . . . ☐

b   **Account Transcript,** which contains information on the financial status of the account, such as payments made on the account, penalty assessments, and adjustments made by you or the IRS after the return was filed. Return information is limited to items such as tax liability and estimated tax payments. Account transcripts are available for most returns. Most requests will be processed within 30 calendar days. . . ☐

c   **Record of Account,** which is a combination of line item information and later adjustments to the account. Available for current year and 3 prior tax years. Most requests will be processed within 30 calendar days . . . . ☐

7   **Verification of Nonfiling,** which is proof from the IRS that you **did not** file a return for the year. Current year requests are only available after June 15th. There are no availability restrictions on prior year requests. Most requests will be processed within 10 business days . ☐

8   **Form W-2, Form 1099 series, Form 1098 series, or Form 5498 series transcript.** The IRS can provide a transcript that includes data from these information returns. State or local information is not included with the Form W-2 information. The IRS may be able to provide this transcript information for up to 10 years. Information for the current year is generally not available until the year after it is filed with the IRS. For example, W-2 information for 2007, filed in 2008, will not be available from the IRS until 2009. If you need W-2 information for retirement purposes, you should contact the Social Security Administration at 1-800-772-1213. Most requests will be processed within 45 days . . . ☐

Caution. *If you need a copy of Form W-2 or Form 1099, you should first contact the payer. To get a copy of the Form W-2 or Form 1099 filed with your return, you must use Form 4506 and request a copy of your return, which includes all attachments.*

9   **Year or period requested.** Enter the ending date of the year or period, using the mm/dd/yyyy format. If you are requesting more than four years or periods, you must attach another Form 4506-T. For requests relating to quarterly tax returns, such as Form 941, you must enter each quarter or tax period separately.

Signature of taxpayer(s). I declare that I am either the taxpayer whose name is shown on line 1a or 2a, or a person authorized to obtain the tax information requested. If the request applies to a joint return, **either** husband or wife must sign. If signed by a corporate officer, partner, guardian, tax matters partner, executor, receiver, administrator, trustee, or party other than the taxpayer, I certify that I have the authority to execute Form 4506-T on behalf of the taxpayer. **Note.** *For transcripts being sent to a third party, this form must be received within 120 days of signature date.*

		Telephone number of taxpayer on line 1a or 2a
Sign Here ▶	Signature (see instructions)	Date
	Title (if line 1a above is a corporation, partnership, estate, or trust)	
▶	Spouse's signature	Date

For Privacy Act and Paperwork Reduction Act Notice, see page 2.   Cat. No. 37667N   Form **4506-T** (Rev. 1-2010)

Making Home Affordable Program
Request For Mortgage Assistance (RMA)

MAKING HOME AFFORDABLE.gov

If you are experiencing a financial hardship and need help, you must complete and submit this form along with other required documentation to be considered for foreclosure prevention options under the Making Home Affordable (MHA) Program. You must provide information about yourself and your intentions to either keep or transition out of your property; a description of the hardship that prevents you from paying your mortgage(s); information about **all** of your income, expenses and financial assets; whether you have declared bankruptcy; and information about the mortgage(s) on your principal residence and other single family real estate that you own. Finally, you will need to return to your loan servicer (1) this completed, signed and dated Request for Mortgage Assistance (RMA); and (2) completed and signed IRS Form 4506-T or 4506T-EZ; and (3) all required income documentation identified in Section 4.

When you sign and date this form, you will make important certifications, representations and agreements, including certifying that all of the information in this RMA is accurate and truthful.

SECTION 1: BORROWER INFORMATION

BORROWER	CO-BORROWER
BORROWER'S NAME Johnny Homeowner	CO-BORROWER'S NAME
SOCIAL SECURITY NUMBER / DATE OF BIRTH (MM/DD/YY) 000-00-0000 05/15/72	SOCIAL SECURITY NUMBER / DATE OF BIRTH (MM/DD/YY)
HOME PHONE NUMBER WITH AREA CODE 222-555-5555	HOME PHONE NUMBER WITH AREA CODE
CELL OR WORK NUMBER WITH AREA CODE	CELL OR WORK NUMBER WITH AREA CODE
MAILING ADDRESS 14562 Elm Street Nowhere California 90065	MAILING ADDRESS (IF SAME AS BORROWER, WRITE "SAME")
EMAIL ADDRESS	EMAIL ADDRESS

Has any borrower filed for bankruptcy? ☐ Chapter 7 ☐ Chapter 13 Filing Date: _____ Bankruptcy case number: _____ Has your bankruptcy been discharged? ☐ Yes ☐ No	Is any borrower a servicemember? ☐ Yes ☒ No Have you recently been deployed away from your principal residence or recently received a permanent change of station order? ☐ Yes ☐ No

How many single family properties other than your principal residence do you and/or any co-borrower(s) own individually, jointly, or with others?   0

Has the mortgage on your principal residence ever had a Home Affordable Modification Program (HAMP) trial period plan or permanent modification? ☐ Yes ☒ No

Has the mortgage on any other property that you or any co-borrower own had a permanent HAMP modification? ☐ Yes ☐ No   If 'Yes', how many? _____

Are you or any co-borrower currently in or being considered for a HAMP trial period plan on a property other than your principal residence? ☐ Yes ☐ No

SECTION 2: HARDSHIP AFFIDAVIT

I (We) am/are requesting review under MHA.
I am having difficulty making my monthly payment because of financial difficulties created by (check all that apply):

☒	My household income has been reduced. For example: reduced pay or hours, decline in business or self employment earnings, death, disability or divorce of a borrower or co-borrower.	☒	My monthly debt payments are excessive and I am overextended with my creditors. Debt includes credit cards, home equity or other debt.
☐	My expenses have increased. For example: monthly mortgage payment reset, high medical or health care costs, uninsured losses, increased utilities or property taxes.	☒	My cash reserves, including all liquid assets, are insufficient to maintain my current mortgage payment and cover basic living expenses at the same time.
☐	I am unemployed and (a) I am receiving/will receive unemployment benefits or (b) my unemployment benefits ended less than 6 months ago.		Other

Explanation (continue on a separate sheet of paper if necessary)

SECTION 3: PRINCIPAL RESIDENCE INFORMATION
(This section is required even if you are not seeking mortgage assistance on your principal residence)

I am requesting mortgage assistance with my principal residence ☒ Yes ☐ No

If "yes", I want to: ☒ Keep the property ☐ Sell the property

Property Address: 14562 Elm Street Nowhere California 90065   Loan I.D. Number: xx-25a2g88

Other mortgages or liens on the property? ☐ Yes ☒ No   Lien Holder / Servicer Name: _____   Loan I.D. Number _____

Do you have condominium or homeowner association (HOA) fees? ☒ Yes ☐ No   If "Yes", Monthly Fee $250.00   Are fees paid current? ☐ Yes ☐ No

Name and address that fees are paid to: Lunkenbill Housing Association

Does your mortgage payment include taxes and Insurance? ☒ Yes ☐ No   If "No", are the taxes and insurance paid current? ☐ Yes ☐ No

Annual Homeowner's Insurance $1200.0

Is the property listed for sale? ☐ Yes ☒ No   If "Yes", Listing Agent's Name: _____   Phone Number _____

List date? _____ Have you received a purchase offer? ☐ Yes ☐ No   Amount of Offer $ _____   Closing Date: _____

Complete this section ONLY if you are requesting mortgage assistance with a property that is not your principal residence.

Principal residence servicer name: _____   Principal residence servicer phone number: _____

Is the mortgage on your principal residence paid? ☐ Yes ☐ No   If 'No', number of months your payment is past due (if known) _____

SECTION 4: COMBINED INCOME AND EXPENSE OF BORROWER AND CO-BORROWER

Monthly Household Income		Monthly Household Expenses/Debt (*Principal Residence Expense Only)		Household Assets	
Monthly Gross wages	$ $3000.00	First Mortgage Principal & Interest Payment*	$ $1950.00	Checking Account(s)	$
Overtime	$	Second Mortgage Principal & Interest Payment*	$	Checking Account(s)	$
Self employment Income	$	Homeowner's Insurance*	$ $1200.00	Savings / Money Market	$
Unemployment Income	$	Property Taxes*	$	CDs	$
Untaxed Social Security / SSD	$	HOA/Condo Fees*	$ $250.00	Stocks / Bonds	$
Food Stamps/Welfare	$	Credit Cards/Installment debt (total min. payment)	$	Other Cash on Hand	$
Taxable Social Security or retirement income	$	Child Support / Alimony	$		
Child Support / Alimony**	$	Car Payments	$ $600.00		
Tips, commissions, bonus and overtime	$	Mortgage Payments other properties****	$ $1200.00		
Gross Rents Received ***	$ $800.00	Other	$	Value of all Real Estate except principal residence	$
Other	$			Other	$
Total (Gross Income)	$ $3800.00	Total Debt/Expenses	$ $5200.00	Total Assets	$

** Alimony, child support or separate maintenance income need not be disclosed if you do not choose to have it considered for repaying your mortgage debt.

*** Include rental income received from all properties you own EXCEPT a property for which you are seeking mortgage assistance in Section 6.

**** Include mortgage payments on all properties you own EXCEPT your principal residence and the property for which you are seeking mortgage assistance in Section 6.

Required Income Documentation
(Your servicer may request additional documentation to complete your evaluation for MHA)

All Borrowers	☒ Include a signed IRS Form 4506-T or 4506T-EZ
☒ Do you earn a wage? Borrower Hire Date (MM/DD/YY) _____ Co-borrower Hire Date (MM/DD/YY) _____	☒ For each borrower who is a salaried employee or hourly wage earner, provide the most recent pay stub(s) that reflects at least 30 days of year-to-date income.
☐ Are you self-employed?	☐ Provide your most recent signed and dated quarterly or year-to date profit and loss statement.
☐ Do you receive tips, commissions, bonuses, housing allowance or overtime?	☐ Describe the type of income, how frequently you receive the income and third party documentation describing the income (e.g., employment contracts or printouts documenting tip income).
☐ Do you receive social security, disability, death benefits, pension, public assistance or adoption assistance?	☐ Provide documentation showing the amount and frequency of the benefits, such as letters, exhibits, disability policy or benefits statement from the provider and receipt of payment (such as two most recent bank statements or deposit advices).
☐ Do you receive alimony, child support, or separation maintenance payments?	☐ Provide a copy of the divorce decree, separation agreement, or other written legal agreement filed with the court that states the amount of the payments and the period of time that you are entitled to receive them. AND ☐ Copies of your two most recent bank statements or deposit advices showing you have received payment. **Notice: Alimony, child support or separate maintenance income need not be disclosed if you do not choose to have it considered for repaying your mortgage debt.**
☒ Do you have income from rental properties that are not your principal residence?	☒ Provide your most recent Federal Tax return with all schedules, including Schedule E. ☒ If rental income is not reported on Schedule E, provide a copy of the current lease agreement with bank statements showing deposit of rent checks.

SECTION 5: OTHER PROPERTIES OWNED

Other Property #1

Property Address: 5620 Gad Street Turtle Arizona   Loan I.D. Number: e66d00

Servicer Name: Dry Gulch Savings and Loan   Mortgage Balance $ 35500.00   Current Value $ 95600.00

Property is: ☐ Vacant ☐ Second or seasonal home ☐ Rented   Gross Monthly Rent $ 800.00   Monthly mortgage payment* $ 800.00

Other Property #2

Property Address: _____   Loan I.D. Number: _____

Servicer Name: _____   Mortgage Balance $ _____   Current Value $ _____

Property is: ☐ Vacant ☐ Second or seasonal home ☐ Rented   Gross Monthly Rent $ _____   Monthly mortgage payment* $ _____

Other Property #3

Property Address: _____   Loan I.D. Number: _____

Servicer Name: _____   Mortgage Balance $ _____   Current Value $ _____

Property is: ☐ Vacant ☐ Second or seasonal home ☐ Rented   Gross Monthly Rent $ _____   Monthly mortgage payment* $ _____

* The amount of the monthly payment made to your lender – including, if applicable, monthly principal, interest, real property taxes and insurance premiums..

Glossary of Modification Terms

Amortization: Repayment of a mortgage loan through monthly installments of principal and interest; the monthly payment amount is based on a schedule that will allow you to own your home at the end of a specific time period (for example, 15 or 30 years)

Annual Percentage Rate (APR): Calculated by using a standard formula, the APR shows the cost of a loan; expressed as a yearly interest rate, it includes the interest, points, mortgage insurance, and other fees associated with the loan.

ARM: Adjustable Rate Mortgage; a mortgage loan subject to changes in interest rates; when rates change, ARM monthly payments increase or decrease at intervals determined by the lender; the change in monthly - payment amount, however, is usually subject to a cap.

Balloon Mortgage: A mortgage loan that requires a large payment due upon maturity (for example, at the end of ten years).

Bankruptcy: A federal law whereby a person's assets are turned over to a trustee and used to pay off outstanding debts; this usually occurs when someone owes more than they have the ability to repay.

Borrower: A person who has been approved to receive a loan and is then obligated to repay it and any additional fees according to the loan terms.

Chapter 13 Bankruptcy: This type of bankruptcy sets a payment plan between the homeowner and the creditor monitored by the bankruptcy court. The homeowner can keep the property, but must make payments according to the court's terms within a three to five year period.

Chapter 7 Bankruptcy: A bankruptcy that requires assets be liquidated in exchange for the cancellation of debt.

Closing: When selling a house, the process of transferring ownership from the seller to the buyer, the disbursement of funds from the buyer and the lender to the seller, and the signing of all the documents associated with the sale and the loan. On a refinance, there is no transfer of ownership, but the closing includes repayment of the old lender.

Co-Homeowners: Persons who have signed a loan note, and are equally responsible for repaying the loan.

Collections: The efforts a lender takes to collect past due payments.

Convertible ARM: An Adjustable Rate Mortgage loan that can be converted into a fixed-rate mortgage during a certain time period.

Credit history: History of an individual's debt payment; lenders use this information to gauge a potential borrower's ability to repay a loan.

Credit report: A record that lists all past and present debts and the timeliness of their repayment; it documents an individual's credit history.

Creditor: A person or entity that is owed money by another person or entity.

Debt-to-income ratio (DTI): A comparison of gross income to housing and non-housing expenses; With the FHA, the-monthly mortgage payment should be no more than 29% of monthly gross income (before taxes) and the mortgage payment combined with non-housing debts should not exceed 41% of income.

Deed: a document that legally transfers ownership of property from one person to another. The deed is recorded on public record with the property description and the owner's signature. Also known as the title.

Deferred Payments: These are loan payments that are authorized to be postponed as part of a workout process to avoid foreclosure.

Deed-in-lieu: To avoid foreclosure ("in lieu" of foreclosure), a deed is given to the lender to fulfill the obligation to repay the debt; this process doesn't allow the borrower to remain in the house but helps avoid the costs, time, and effort associated with foreclosure.

Delinquency: Failure of a borrower to make timely mortgage payments under a loan agreement.

Equity: An owner's financial interest in a property, calculated by subtracting the amount still owed on the mortgage loan(s) from the fair market value of the property.

Escrow Account: A separate account into which a portion of each monthly mortgage payment is placed; an escrow account provides the funds needed for such expenses as property taxes, homeowners insurance, mortgage insurance, etc.

Escrow Analysis: A periodic review of escrow accounts to make sure that there are sufficient funds to pay the taxes and insurance on a home when they are due.

Fair market value: The hypothetical price that a willing buyer and seller will agree upon when they are acting freely, carefully, and with complete knowledge of the situation.

First mortgage: A mortgage that has a first-priority claim against the property in the event the homeowner defaults on the loan.

Fixed-rate mortgage: A mortgage with payments that remain the same throughout the life of the loan because the interest rate and other terms are fixed and do not change.

Foreclosure: A legal process in which mortgaged property is sold to pay the loan of the defaulting borrower.

Foreclosure Prevention: The steps by which the servicer works with the homeowner to find a permanent solution to resolve an existing or impending loan delinquency.

Forbearance: A loss mitigation option where the lender arranges a revised repayment plan for the borrower that may include a temporary reduction or suspension of monthly loan payments.

Government Sponsored Enterprises (GSE): The government sponsored enterprises (GSEs) are a group of financial services corporations created by the United States Congress. Their function is to enhance the flow of credit to targeted sectors of the economy and to make those segments of the capital market more efficient and transparent. The desired effect of the GSEs is to enhance the availability and reduce the cost of credit to the targeted borrowing sectors: agriculture, home finance and education.

Good faith estimate (GFE): An estimate of all closing fees including pre-paid and escrow items as well as lender charges; must be given to the borrower within three days after submission of a loan application.

HAFA Short Sale: When the homeowner sells the property for less than the full amount due on the mortgage. When a homeowner qualifies for the HAFA short sale, the servicer approves the short sale terms prior to listing the home and then accepts the payoff in full satisfaction of the mortgage.

Home Affordable Foreclosure Alternatives Program (HAFA): A program that provides opportunities for homeowners who can no longer afford to stay in their home but want to avoid foreclosure to transition to more affordable housing through a short sale or deed-in-lieu of foreclosure

Home Affordable Modification Program (HAMP): A program that provides eligible homeowners the opportunity to modify their mortgages to make them more affordable.

Home Affordable Refinance Program (HARP): A program that provides homeowners with loans owned or guaranteed by Fannie Mae or Freddie Mac an opportunity to refinance into more affordable monthly payments.

Home Affordable Unemployment Program (UP): A program that provides homeowners a temporary forbearance, which is a temporary period of time during which a regular monthly mortgage payment is reduced or suspended.

Hard expenses: Hard expenses are monthly expenses that are definite and documented. Examples include installment debt like mortgage payments, car loans, and personal loans. Most hard expenses will be included on one's credit report.

Hazard Insurance: Insurance that is generally required under mortgage contracts to pay for loss or damage to a person's home or property.

Home Equity Line of Credit (HELOC): A way of borrowing money against the equity in one's home to pay for things such as home repairs, college education, or other personal uses.

Housing expense: The sum of a homeowner's mortgage payment, hazard insurance, property taxes, and homeowner association fees.

Interest: A fee charged for the use of money.

Interest rate: The amount of interest charged on a monthly loan payment expressed as a percentage.

Interest Only: A feature of some MLCC loan programs that allows the borrower to pay only the interest on a loan, without paying down any principal with each monthly payment.

Investment Property: A property not considered to be a primary residence that is purchased in order to generate income, profit from appreciation, or to take advantage of certain tax benefits.

Lender: To give/lend money on condition that it is returned and that interest is paid for its temporary use. Banks are commonly known as lenders. Your mortgage broker is not a lender, but rather sold your loan to a lender.

Lender-Placed Insurance: Insurance placed on a home or property by a lender to protect their interest in the collateral which secures the loan.

Lien: A legal claim against property that must be satisfied when the property is sold.

Loan-to-value Ratio (LTV): A percentage calculated by dividing the amount borrowed by the price or appraised value of the home to be purchased; the higher the LTV, the less cash a borrower is required to pay as down payment.

Loss mitigation: A process to avoid foreclosure; the lender tries to help a borrower who has been unable to make loan payments and is in danger of defaulting on his or her loan.

Monthly Gross Income: The total incomes of all homeowners who sign a mortgage before any taxes or other deductions are made.

Mortgage (Mortgage Backed Security): A lien on the property that secures the Promise to repay a loan.

Mortgage Banker: A company that originates loans and resells them to secondary mortgage lenders like Fannie Mae or Freddie Mac.

Mortgage Broker: A firm that originates and processes loans for a number of lenders.

Mortgage Insurance: A policy that protects lenders against some or most of the losses that can occur when a borrower defaults on a mortgage loan; mortgage insurance is required primarily for borrowers with a down payment of less than 20% of the home's purchase price.

Mortgage Modification: A change in the terms of a loan, usually the interest rate and/or term, in response to the homeowner's inability to make the payments under the existing contract.

Mortgage Payment: The amount of money paid on a monthly basis for principal, interest, property taxes, hazard insurance and homeowner's association fees, if applicable.

Mortgage Payment Guideline: The calculation within HAMP that helps determine a homeowner's eligibility. It is calculated as 31% of the homeowner's current monthly gross income. If the monthly mortgage payment is above this amount, a homeowner may be eligible for HAMP.

Negative Equity: The condition of owing more on the property than the property is worth

Payment To Income Ratio (PTI): Lenders use what is called a front-end ratio, which is reflected as a percentage of your gross monthly income. The front-end ratio signifies the payment a buyer can reasonably afford, from a lender's point of view. You may prefer a lower payment.

The front-end ratio for a FHA loan is 31%. For a conforming conventional loan, the front-end ratio is 33%. This means if your monthly gross income is $4,000, to qualify for the maximum FHA loan, your monthly principal, interest, taxes and insurance (PITI) payment cannot exceed $1,240. For a conventional loan, it is $1,320.

PITIA: Shorthand for principal, interest, taxes and insurance, which are the components of the housing expense.

Pre-foreclosure: A sale when the servicer allows the homeowner to list and sell the mortgaged property with the understanding that the net proceeds from the sale may be less than the total amount due on the first mortgage. Also referred to as a "short sale."

Primary or Principal Residence: The property in which the homeowner will live most of the time, as distinct from a second home or an investor property that will be rented.

Principal Balance Reduction: Instance where the bank forgives a portion of your principal balance as part of a loan modification. The mortgage payment due for this note is based off the new loan amount. Only applicable in heavily depreciated areas.

Private-Label Mortgages: Loans that are not owned or guaranteed by Fannie Mae, Freddie Mac, Ginnie Mae, or another Federal agency.

Refinancing: Paying off one loan by obtaining another; refinancing is generally done to secure better loan terms (like a lower interest rate).

Repayment Plan: Adding a portion of the delinquent mortgage balance on top of the normal monthly payments until caught up.

RESPA: Real Estate Settlement Procedures Act A federal consumer protection statute supervised and enforced by the Department of Housing and Urban Development (HUD). First passed in 1974, it requires various disclosures in order to help consumers make more informed decisions when shopping for settlement (real estate closing) services. It also seeks to eliminate kickbacks and referral fees, which unnecessarily increase the costs of certain settlement services. It applies to mortgage loans on single-family housing, duplexes, triplexes, and four-plexus (generally described as "one- to four-family residential property"), whether the loan is for a purchase, refinance, property improvement, or home equity line of credit.

Second Lien Modification Program (2MP): A program that provides homeowners a way to modify their second mortgages to make them more affordable when their first mortgage is modified under the HAMP.

Second Mortgage: A loan with a second-priority claim against a property in the event that the homeowner defaults. The lender who holds the second mortgage gets paid only after the lender holding the first mortgage is paid.

Servicer: A firm that works on behalf of the lender in support of a mortgage, including collecting mortgage payments, ensuring payment of taxes and insurance, managing escrow accounts, managing communications with the homeowner, and loss mitigation or foreclosure when necessary.

Servicing Transfer: When one servicer is replaced by another.

Short Sale: A sale of a house in which the proceeds fall short of what the owner still owes on the mortgage. Many lenders will agree to accept the proceeds of a short sale and forgive the rest of what is owed on the mortgage when the owner cannot make the mortgage payments. By accepting a short sale, the lender can avoid a lengthy and costly foreclosure, and the owner is able to pay off the loan for less than what he owes.

Soft Expenses: Monthly expenses that fluctuate and are difficult to document. These include food, gas, incidentals, entertainment and are not reported on one's credit report.

Teaser Rate: A temporary rate reduction at the inset of a loan.

TILA: The Truth in Lending Act applies to most types of credit, whether it be closed-end credit (such as an auto loan or mortgage), or open-ended credit (such as a credit card). The act regulates what companies can advertise and say about the benefits of their loans or services. For example, borrowers considering an adjustable-rate mortgage must be offered specific reading materials from the Federal Reserve Board to ensure they understand the parameters of an ARM.

Different states and industries have their own variations of TILA, but the chief feature remains the proper disclosure of key information to protect both the consumer and the lender in credit transactions.

Title: The documented evidence that a person or organization has ownership of real property.

Trial Period or Trial Period Plan: HAMP requires homeowners to enter into a trial period plan before receiving a permanent HAMP modification. During this period, homeowners must submit all required trial period payments. The trial period is at minimum, a three or four month period to see if the new reduced payment is sustainable, while providing relief and preventing any possible foreclosure sales from occurring. During the trial period, the terms and conditions of the original loan remain unchanged, and only after all trial payments are made on time and all documents are submitted and verified can the loan be permanently modified.

Trust: A relationship in which one person holds title to property, subject to an obligation to keep or use the property for the benefit of another.

Underwriting: Is a process of examining all the data about a homeowner's property and income documentation to determine whether the mortgage modification should be issued. The person who does this is called an underwriter.

Unpaid Principal Balance (UPB): amount of a loan that is due to the lender. This does not include additional charges, such as interest.

Weighted Average Life: This is a calculation in which the average number of years for which each dollar of unpaid principal on a loan or mortgage remains outstanding.

Work Out: A way to resolve or restructure a loan to prevent a homeowner from going into foreclosure through a loan modification, forbearance or short sale.

Lenders who participate in HAMP

The following chart shows the current lenders, as of 2015, who are participating with the Making Home Affordable Program

Allstate Mortgage Loans & Investments, Inc.	866-351-0200
Amarillo National Bank	806-378-8000
American Financial Resources Inc.	800-316-9508
AMS Servicing, LLC	866-919-5608
Aurora Financial Group, Inc.	800-648-0345
Aurora Loan Services LLC	800-550-0508
Banco Popular de Puerto Rico	787-775-1100
Bank of America, N.A. (Includes: Countrywide Home Loans Servicing LP, Home Loan Services, Inc.)	800-720-3758
Bank United	866-615-0662
Bay view Loan Servicing, LLC	800-457-5105
Capital International Financial, Inc.	305-442-1256
Carrington Mortgage Services, LLC	888-267-2417
CCO Mortgage	877-745-7366
Central Florida Educators Federal Credit Union	800-771-9411
CitiMortgage, Inc.	866-915-9417
Citizens 1st National Bank	800-311-7531
Community Bank & Trust Company	
CU Mortgage Services, Inc.	651-631-3111
CUC Mortgage Corporation	800-342-4998

DuPage Credit Union	800-323-2611
Fay Servicing, LLC	800-495-7166
Fidelity Homestead Savings Bank	504-569-3490
First Bank	800-760-2265
First Federal Bank of Florida	386-754-0090
First Financial Bank, N.A.	812-238-6311
First Mortgage Corporation	800-395-4778
Flagstar	800-968-7700
Franklin Credit Management Corporation	800-255-5897
Franklin Savings	513-469-8000
Gateway Mortgage Group, LLC	918-712-9000
Glass City Federal Credit Union	800-837-3595
GMAC Mortgage LLC	800-766-4622
Great Lakes Credit Union	800-442-3488
Greater Nevada Mortgage Services	800-421-6674
Green Tree Servicing LLC	800-643-0202
Guaranty Bank	800-235-4636
Hartford Savings Bank	800-844-3812
Hillsdale County National Bank	517-439-6121
HomEq Servicing	877-867-7378
Homeward Residential	877-304-3100
Horicon Bank	920-485-3080 ext. 7310
IBM Lender Business Processing Services	866-570-5277
IC Federal Credit Union	800-262-1001
Idaho Housing and Finance Association	208-331-4726

iServe Residential Lending, LLC	888-875-8326
iServe Servicing, Inc.	888-858-7378
J.P. Morgan Chase Bank, NA (includes: Chase Home Finance, LLC and EMC Mortgage Corporation)	
	866-550-5705
James B. Nutter & Company	800-798-3946
Lake City Bank	888-522-2265
Liberty Bank and Trust Co	800-883-3943
Litton Loan Servicing	800-247-9727
Los Alamos National Bank	800-684-5262
M&T Bank	800-724-1633
Magna Bank	800-553-0558
Marix Servicing, LLC	866-406-2749
Marsh Associates, Inc.	800-553-0558
Midland Mortgage Company	800-552-3000
Midwest Community Bank	815-235-6137
Mission Federal Credit Union	800-500-6328 x2074
Mortgage Center, LLC	866-856-3750
National City Bank	800-523-8654
Nationstar Mortgage LLC	888-850-9398
Navy Federal Credit Union	888-842-6328
Ocean Financial Corporation, Inc.	800-746-2936
One West Bank	800-781-7399
ORNL Federal Credit Union	800-676-5328
Pathfinder Bank	315-343-0057

Penny Mac Loan Services, LLC	866-601-3518
PNC Bank, National Association	800-523-8654
Purdue Employees Federal Credit Union	800-627-3328
Q lending, Inc.	517-439-6121
Quantum Servicing Corporation	813-371-0270
RBC Bank (USA)	866-777-2179
Residential Credit Solutions	800-737-1192
RG Mortgage Corporation	888-264-4674
Round Point Mortgage Servicing Corporation	877-426-8805
Saxon Mortgage Services	800-594-8422
Schmidt Mortgage Company	800-686-3600
Schools Financial Credit Union	800-962-0990
Select Portfolio Servicing	888-818-6032
Servis One Inc.,dba BSI Financial Services, Inc.	866-209-4178
ShoreBank	800-905-7725
Silver State Schools Credit Union	800-357-9654
Specialized Loan Servicing, LLC	800-315-4757
Sterling Savings Bank	800-772-7791
Stockman Bank of Montana	406-234-8420
Technology Credit Union	800-553-0880
The Golden 1 Credit Union	800-553-0880
U.S. Bank National Association	866-932-0462
United Bank	715-835-6865
United Bank Mortgage Corporation	800-968-1990
Vantium Capital, Inc.	866-660-5804

Vista Financial Corp.	
Wealthbridge Mortgage Corp.	866-702-4865
Wells Fargo Bank, NA (includes: Wachovia Bank, NA and Wachovia Mortgage, FSB)	800-678-7986
Weststar Mortgage, Inc.	703-497-3995
Yadkin Valley Bank	336-258-6252

APPENDIX

Affordable, M. H. (2013). Viewing Programs of Making Home Affordable. Retrieved May 2013, from MakingHomeaffordable.com: http://www.makinghomeaffordable.gov/programs/view-all-programs/Pages/default.aspx

Hardship Letter Form. (n.d.). Retrieved May 2013, from Bank of America: http://homeloanhelp.bankofamerica.com/en/assets/documents/Hardship-Letter_Bank-of-America.pdf

IRS. (n.d.). Mortgage Forgiveness Debt Relief Act 2007. Retrieved from http://www.irs.gov/Individuals/The-Mortgage-Forgiveness-Debt-Relief-Act-and-Debt-Cancellation

Revenue, I. (2013, May 2013). Extension of Time To File Your Tax Return. Retrieved from http://www.irs.gov/uac/Extension-of-Time-To-File-Your-Tax-Return

ABOUT THE AUTHOR

For the past 18 years, in both the United States, and in Great Brittan, Reuben Dunn has been assisting clients with their credit consolidation concerns, debt counseling and consumer credit finance.

For four of these years Reuben has worked exclusively with homeowners seeking modification assistance for their mortgages, as well as walking them through the stages of short sale, and, occasionally, walking them through the process of foreclosure.

Reuben is licensed in real estate, in the State of California, and is a Real Estate Consultant, working for one of the largest Real Estate brokers in the United States.

He currently resides in Utah, working in the mortgage services industry, and is the father of three children, two of whom are married.

www.ingramcontent.com/pod-product-compliance
Lightning Source LLC
Chambersburg PA
CBHW022044190326
41520CB00008B/701